is
a Living Spirit

Translated from the French
Original title: « LA LUMIÈRE, ESPRIT VIVANT »

Original edition:
© 1983, Éditions Prosveta S.A. (France), ISBN 2-85566-235-4

© 1983, Éditions Prosveta S.A. , ISBN 2-85566-252-4
© 1984, Éditions Prosveta S.A. , ISBN 2-85566-278-8
© 1986, Éditions Prosveta S.A. , ISBN 2-85566-391-1

Prosveta S.A – B.P.12 – 83601 Fréjus CEDEX (France)

ISSN 0763-2738
ISBN 978-2-85566-391-3

Omraam Mikhaël Aïvanhov

Light
is
a Living Spirit

Izvor Collection – No. 212

PROSVETA

Readers are asked to note that Omraam Mikhaël Aïvanhov's teaching was exclusively oral. This volume includes passages from several different lectures all dealing with the same theme.

TABLE OF CONTENTS

Chapter One

LIGHT: THE ESSENCE OF CREATION

It has been said that God is a consuming fire, and in most mythologies, the god of fire was the most powerful of all the gods. We are not speaking here, of course, of the fire which burns in our hearths; physical fire is only one aspect of the universal Fire. Actually, there are many different kinds of fire: the fire that burns in the hearts of men, the fire that slumbers at the base of the spine, the fire of the sun, the fire of hell, the fire hidden in stone and metal, etc.

Have you ever realized that fire is visible only if it is accompanied by light? This is because light is the matter by means of which fire manifests itself. And if we transpose this image onto a higher plane we find that light is the substance which emanated from God, the primordial Fire, at the beginning of the world, when He said, *'Let there be light'*. It is this Light which St John, in the Prologue to his *Gospel*, calls the *'Word'*: *'In the beginning was the Word, and the Word was with God, and the*

Word was God... All things were made through Him...' Light is the Word uttered by the Creator and by means of this Light He created the world.

The physical world, as we know it, is simply the condensation of that primordial Light. God, the active principle, emitted Light and used that Light as the raw material out of which He created the universe. And it is here that one gets a first glimpse of the two principles, masculine and feminine, which are at the origin of the created universe: God, the primordial Fire, the masculine principle, drew from within Himself and projected outwards the feminine principle, Light, the matter with which He created.

We are told that God created the world out of nothing. If we understand by that that He used nothing from outside Himself, then this is true, and it is this that is so difficult to understand, for we human beings can create only by using materials and tools which are not ourselves. The truth is that it is not possible to create something out of nothing; to say that God created out of nothing simply means that God drew the raw materials of creation from Himself. The universe, therefore, is God's very own substance; it came from Him, it has become exterior to Him, and yet it is still Him.[1]

What does the silkworm use to spin its cocoon, the spider to spin its web or the snail to make its shell? They all draw a substance from themselves.

If you know how to look at nature properly you will see a great many phenomena which can throw light on questions which thinkers consider to be the deepest and most unfathomable mysteries. One day, in fact, even scientists will discover that light is the primordial matter from which the universe was created, and if man learns how to set about it, he too will be able to create, like God.

According to the *Book of Genesis*, the very first event in the world was the creation of Light. God said, *'Let there be light'*. But what was this light? In Bulgarian there are two different words for light, *svetlina* and *videlina*. *Svetlina* designates physical light and has the same root as the verb which means 'to shine', whereas *videlina* designates spiritual light and is formed from the root of the verb which means 'to see'. *Videlina* is the light which enables us to see the spiritual, invisible world; it was *videlina* that was condensed into material form and gave us svetlina, physical light.

Perhaps you will understand this better if you think of a Crookes tube: at each end of the tube in which a vacuum has been created is an electrode connected to a source of electrical current. When the current is switched on, the cathode emits a flow of electrons in the direction of the anode, with the result that the immediate vicinity of the anode is illuminated, although the cathode itself remains dark.

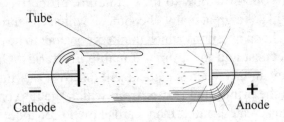

A Crookes Tube

The light that we receive from the sun is not the Light of that first day of creation of which *Genesis* speaks. Beyond the visible sun is the invisible, dark Sun which pours a ceaseless stream of energies into our visible sun, and the visible sun transforms them and sends them on in the form of light. The light that we see is not that which God created on the first day, when He said, *'Let there be light'*. The light that we see came later. The first sun emitted the primordial Light, *videlina*, which the visible sun transforms and sends out as rays of visible light *(svetlina)*. *Videlina*, true Light, only lights up objects that cross its path; if it encounters no obstacle it remains invisible. The presence of true Light, then, is revealed by the obstacles in its path.

In the beginning was *videlina*, that first movement within the spirit of God which manifested itself by blazing forth, radiating from the centre to the periphery; that first movement outwards from within. Before creating, God encompassed Himself in a circle of light which we may call His aura. The limits of this circle were to become the limits of the universe, and once they were established, God projected into the luminous circle of *videlina*, His aura, images which then crystallized and took on material form, and in this way *videlina* supplied the matter of creation. And when St John says, at the beginning of his *Gospel, 'In the beginning was the Word, and the Word was with God, and the Word was God'*, *'the Word was with God'* means that nothing was created without the participation of *videlina*, God's aura. The divine Word is Light.

We can witness this same process of creation as it is enacted by initiates. They, too, possess a luminous aura which not only surrounds and protects them, but also provides the matter for their creations.[2] When an initiate wishes to create by means of his thoughts, he uses the same methods which God used in creating the universe: he projects an image or pronounces a few words and these projections, as they pass through his aura, take from it the matter they need to manifest themselves. The images or words clothe themselves, as it were, in the matter of the aura. Someone who wants to give concrete form to an idea but who does not possess this subtle matter of the aura can never create anything. You have probably all experienced this: there are days when,

however eloquent you may be, your words have no
effect on people; your audience remains completely
cold and unmoved, whereas on other days, on the
contrary, a few simple words produce a striking
impression. The reason is that those few words
were alive; before they reached their target they
had been steeped in your aura from which they had
drawn life and strength; thus made powerful they
were able to reach the souls of others and cause
them to vibrate. On the days when your aura is
weak, your words will be meaningless and empty;
there is nothing there. You speak, but with no
effect. Your words are not impregnated with that
element which only the aura can give, *videlina*.

The power of initiates comes from the fact that
they know how to impregnate their words with the
pure, abundant, intense matter of their aura. The
spoken word is only a vehicle or support, it can
only take effect if it is steeped in the creative
element, *videlina*. Someone who does not understand how to speak magic words can shout and
gesticulate as much as he likes, but he will never
be heard by the higher spirits nor persuade them to
come to his help. But an initiate who quietly utters
the same words, without a single gesture, simply
by the inner power derived from his aura, will
obtain mighty results.

It was not the spoken word which created the
world, it was the Logos, the divine Word, Light.

The Logos was the first element to be set in motion by God, and the spoken word is the medium which the divine Word uses in Its work of creation. When that primeval force came forth from God it was spirit; it became light as it returned to God. The dark sun sends *videlina*, the spirit, to the bright, visible sun, and the bright sun sends it back to the dark sun in the form of visible light, *svetlina*. The spirit becomes light as it returns to God. When God initiated the first movement, His Spirit, the Word, was set in motion, and when It returned to God It had become light. Whatever goes out from the centre to the periphery, returns to the centre once it has reached the limits of the circle, and in this way a continual ebb and flow, a circular movement, is set in motion from the centre to the outer periphery and from the periphery back to the centre. On its return journey towards the centre, the current of forces is invested with new and different qualities and provokes new and different reactions as it goes. Its nature is not the same on the way out as on the way back.

'*In the beginning was the Word*', the first movement of the divine Spirit who created the circle of the universe. In the same way, before a magus performs a magical rite, he forms a circle around himself. The origin of this custom, which dates from very ancient times, is to be found in the secret science concerning the human aura. When

we read that a magus must stand within the circle
he has drawn, this does not mean, simply, that he
must draw a material circle on the ground and stand
within it. It means that he must create the living
circle of his aura and take up his stand within it. In
other words, his spirit must be active and watchful,
otherwise he runs the risk of falling a prey to
invisible entities. If a magus is content to draw a
material circle round himself but has not lived in
such a way as to develop a pure, brilliant, powerful
aura, he may, perhaps, get what he wanted from the
ceremony, but when he steps out of his magic
circle, all those entities who obeyed him while he
was in it (for the invisible entities respect the
symbol of the circle and obey the magic formulas
pronounced by a magus) will cluster round him to
pursue and harass him.

Any magician who is unaware of these laws
will have problems of this kind. The invisible
entities, who are well aware that his aura is neither
pure nor luminous, will end by revenging
themselves on him for forcing them to obey him in
spite of his unworthiness. Magicians of this kind do
not know that in the beginning is the Word. They do
not know, in other words, that before launching into
all kinds of bold undertakings, they should build up
an aura, a true magic circle of light. But this circle
cannot be drawn automatically, with a piece of
chalk or any other material means; it can only be

created by love, purity and selflessness. Why do you suppose that so many people who embark upon the practice of magic not only fail to get any results, but seem to become prone to all kinds of mishaps? It is because their aura is not sufficiently powerful, luminous and pure, so when they try to project a thought they have no materials with which to clothe it or make it strong. If you want a thought to take flight you have to give it wings, and those wings can only be found in your aura.

'In the beginning was the Word, and the Word was with God, and the Word was God.' When God created this great luminous circle He impregnated it with His own essence.[3] Trees, plants, animals and men were all, at one time, images floating in God's aura. Everything that exists, exists in the aura of God. As St Paul puts it: *'In Him we live and move and have our being.'* We are all immersed in God's aura; it permeates and pervades every particle and fibre of our being.

Meditate every day on the power of *videlina*, that living Light that is the primordial element of all creation.

One of the symbols of the creation of the world is the mystical Rose.

The six circles of the petals represent the six days during which God created the world (six symbolic 'days' which lasted billions of years!).

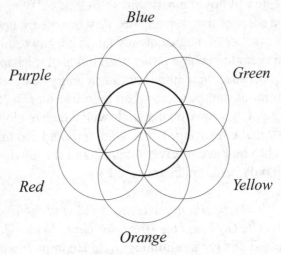

Blue

Purple

Green

Red

Yellow

Orange

Certain esoterics think that the first word of the *Book of Genesis*, *Bereshith*, comes from the verb *bara*, 'to create' and *shith*, 'six.' Put one of the six colours in each circle (purple, blue, green, yellow, orange and red) and meditate on them. The central circle represents the white light which is the source of all the other colours. Even if you have not really grasped the deep symbolic significance of this perfect figure, the very fact of contemplating and meditating on it creates a bond between yourself and it which will help you in your spiritual work.

Light is matter in its subtlest, most tenuous form, and what we call matter is simply highly condensed, concentrated light. In every zone and

region of the universe, therefore, we have the same
fundamental matter – or the same light – in varying
degrees of condensation or subtlety. Everything
that exists on earth in a solid, condensed state,
exists also on the etheric plane in a more refined,
purer form. And this is the whole point of our
spiritual work: to learn how to find all the things
we need in that subtler, finer state which most
nearly resembles their primordial state.[4]

When we go to watch the sun rising in the
morning, this is what we are doing: nourishing
ourselves with the purest of all foods, light. When
Jesus said, *'Blessed are those who hunger and
thirst...'* he was not thinking of physical hunger
and thirst. He was speaking of the hunger and thirst
for truth, wisdom, justice and freedom, of that
ultimate hunger and thirst which ask only for fire
and light.

The soul hungers and the spirit thirsts. The soul
consumes fire and the spirit light. Fire is a masculine principle and the soul is feminine, and every
being is nourished by its complementary element.
The soul yearns for a positive, active, dynamic
principle: it feeds on fire. The spirit, on the other
hand, is masculine; it needs the feminine principle,
so it drinks light. And just as the masculine
principle engenders the feminine principle, so fire
engenders light. Light is a manifestation, an
emanation of fire. When you light a fire it produces

light, and the purer the fuel of that fire, the purer
and subtler the light it produces.

Light is the raiment of fire and this is why light
is always associated with matter. In the sublime
regions on high, light is related to matter and fire
to the spirit. This is why God, the primordial Fire,
first created Light, and Light then created the
world; nothing that was made was made without
Light. Every time you light a fire the story of the
creation of the world is being re-enacted before
your eyes.[5]

Notes

1. See *Angels and other Mysteries of The Tree of Life,* Izvor
   Coll. n° 236, chap. 6: 'Ain Soph Aur, unlimited light'.
2. See *Notre peau spirituelle, l'aura,* Brochure n° 309.
3. See *Angels and other Mysteries of The Tree of Life,* Izvor
   Coll. n° 236, chap. 8: 'When god drew a circle on the face
   of the deep'.
4. See *The Splendour of Tiphareth – The Yoga of the Sun,*
   Complete Works, vol. 10, chap. 1: 'All that exists on earth
   exists etherically in the sun' and chap. 2: 'Obtaining etheric
   elements from the sun'.
5. See *The Mysteries of Fire and Water,* Izvor Coll. n° 232,
   chap. 14: 'How to light and tend fire'.

Chapter Two

THE SUN'S RAYS,
THEIR NATURE AND ACTIVITY

The source of visible light is the sun. But what exactly is the sun? Physicists say that it is a kind of giant incinerator, at the centre of which the temperature is about fifteen million degrees, and that this heat is produced by a constant process of atomic fusion in which hydrogen is transformed into helium. In fact, though, only the great initiates who have the power of projecting their astral bodies into space have actually been to the sun and the other planets and have firsthand knowledge of what they really are. I have often spoken to you about the sun and, in particular, I have told you that modern science tells us that sunbeams are streams of photons, but that initiates see them as tiny wagons laden with food. Sunbeams do not arrive on earth empty-handed: wherever they go throughout space, they take with them all the elements necessary to the life and growth of plants, animals and men, but they also convey many much subtler elements that we can use to further our spiritual development.

Yes, sunbeams can be compared to miniature wagons carrying supplies of food. In an extraordinary, circular flow of traffic, they come down to earth at a tremendous speed, empty themselves of their precious load, and return to the sun by an invisible route. And these wagons carry not only supplies but also passengers, beings who have been sent to earth for some particular task and, when it is done, they too return to the sun to recuperate and refresh themselves. All this is new to you, isn't it?

But there is something else that you don't know either, and that is that this circulation of the sun's rays in space finds its replica in man.[1] Our heart is the sun, and it sends wagonfuls of rays out into the different regions of the physical body and its millions upon millions of citizens. When the wagons reach their destination they unload their supplies and, as they have inevitably lost something of their initial purity, before going back to the sun they follow a circuitous route to purify themselves and get rid of the wastes accumulated on the way. The circulation of the blood in the veins and arteries of our bodies is simply a reflection of the circulation of sunlight in space. For the solar system is a body: the sun is the heart and light is the blood which this heart pumps out to the members and organs of the body for their nourishment. The rays of the sun reach out into space and touch the earth and the other planets, their oceans, their atmosphere and all the creatures that dwell therein, and supply them with everything they need.

Each ray of sunshine is a source of energy. For this reason, when man's other sources of energy: coal, oil, uranium, and so on, are exhausted, he will turn more and more to the energy of the sun, for its resources are limitless. But the energy contained in sunlight is not purely utilitarian: Light is a living Spirit which comes from the sun and which establishes a direct relationship with our own spirit.

When a ray of sunshine strikes an object, whatever it may be, it gives it something. Even the stones on the ground need the life they receive from the sun, for although they are inanimate they have a form of life. This life is more readily perceptible in plants, which grow and reproduce thanks to the action of sunlight, whereas in animals the sun's rays are transformed not only into vitality but also into a form of sensitivity. The fact that animals have a rudimentary perception of suffering and joy is due to the action of the sun's rays. And finally, in man, the sun's rays are transformed into intelligence, for it is only in man that light finds a host sufficiently receptive to enable it to manifest itself as thought. The spirit which speaks through the mouth of man is an emanation of solar light. It is light that thinks, speaks, sings and creates, and as it gradually clears a passage for itself within the human soul, light is reflected in the form of intelligence, love, beauty, nobility and strength.

The sun's rays are the only things that are capable of sustaining, nourishing and increasing the flow of life in man, but he has to learn to absorb them. If you open yourselves wholeheartedly to the action of the sun's rays you will feel that they begin to work for your regeneration and resurrection.

If you want really to sense the power of the sun's rays, to feel the full force of their purity and their godliness, you must continually prepare yourselves in advance, every day, for your encounter with them. If you don't prepare yourselves, you will be just like all the other ignorant, comatose human beings who let the sun's rays pass them by without realizing what wealth they contain. And then they moan and complain: 'I'm hungry and thirsty, weak and destitute. There's no light in my darkness. Won't anyone help me?' And yet everything they need is there, in the sun's rays. Ah, if you only knew those who send us those rays! Yes, the sun is peopled with creatures who are far superior to us, and they look down at us; sometimes they smile at us, and we...? Well, where are we? I know that it is very difficult to get human beings to admit that light is anything more than a physical wave. Their minds are closed to the notion that Light is a living Spirit, and it is for this reason that they are not capable of receiving all the benefits the sun could give them.

You must organize your lives in such a way that light plays an increasingly large part in them. But, more important still, you must become constantly aware that it is already present in all created things, and in this way you will be in a position to benefit from it more fully. If you are conscious of the fact that the cereals, fruit and vegetables you eat are a condensed form of the sunlight to which they were exposed as they were growing, you will be creating the ideal physiological conditions for those rays to be absorbed and diffused throughout your body.[2] If you breathe, convinced that with every breath you are drawing light into yourself, you will be preparing yourself to receive that other light, the Light from heaven, the Spirit of God.[3] For, as I have already said, we must not forget that the visible light of the sun is only the most material form of light. Above and beyond the light we see, are other, subtler forms of light which, if you know how to make contact with them, can bring you the gift of eternal life.

In the morning, when you contemplate the rising sun, remember that those rays of light are living creatures who can help you to solve all the problems of the day ahead. But only that day's problems, not those of the next day or the day after! The next day you must go and seek their advice again and, once again, only for a day at a time. They will never give you solutions for two or three days in advance. They will simply say, 'Don't worry! Come back tomorrow and we'll give you an answer then.' After all, you eat every day, don't you? You don't store up provisions in your stomach for a week; only for the day. Today you eat for today, and tomorrow you will eat for tomorrow. And it should be the same thing with light, for light is a food which you must absorb and digest every single day so that it can become thoughts, feelings and inspirations within you. You are quite logical about your food; why not extend the same logic to light? You would say, 'True, I ate yesterday, but that was for yesterday. I want to eat again today.' Light, like food, has to nourish you every single day.

Why not get into the habit of doing this exercise, for example? You are sitting there, waiting for the first ray of sunlight to appear, wide awake and attentive. As soon as the first rays appear, you begin to drink them, to draw them into yourself. You imagine that you are drinking the sun! Instead of just looking at it and breathing it in, you eat and drink it, thinking all the time of the light that is spreading through all the cells of your organs to strengthen, vivify and purify them. This exercise is a great help when you are trying to concentrate, and it can have truly fantastic results: your whole being will vibrate and you will begin to feel that you are really and truly drinking light.

Thousands of years ago, the sacred scriptures of India revealed the great importance that their sages attributed to the sun. Take the example of the Puranas.

In the Agni Purana, the sun is considered to be the manifestation of Visnu and the universal Source of all that is.

The Matsya Purana says that when we adore the sun we adore Brahma, Visnu and Siva, the trinity which corresponds to the Father, Son and Holy Spirit of the Christian religions.

In the Markandeya Purana, the sun is called 'Abode of Knowledge', 'Cleanser of Darkness', 'Stainless and supreme Soul', 'universal Cause', 'Material and Non-material', and is considered to be the primeval Power which exists in all forms of water, earth, wind and fire. It also teaches that he who reverently adores the sun every morning, in humility and tranquillity, obtains the grace of Laksmi, goddess of love and beauty. Those who adore the sun with undivided attention are delivered from sin and enjoy immunity from all disease.

The Brahma Purana describes the sun as the 'Eye of the three Worlds', 'Lord of the Universe, 'Germ of Action', 'Harbour of Mercy' and as the symbol of action itself.

The Brahmanda Purana says that the sun is the cause of all activities in the world.

The Linga Purana states that the sun is the universal order.

The Padma Purana gives some Tantric hymns to be used in sun worship so that all mental and physical disease may be cured.

In the Brahma-vaivarta Purana it is said that the sun cures all disease and releases men from sorrow, mental agitation and fear. He bestows on men happiness, redemption, faith and every kind of blessing.

Throughout the ages, initiatic science has always considered the physical sun as the sign and symbol of the true spiritual sun, Centre of universal Knowledge and universal Power, manifested in the seven rays of light. This is why, if you want my advice, you must leave everything else to one side and devote all your attention to the study of the sun's rays. If you only knew the power, wealth, light, purity and intelligence contained in just one little ray of sunlight! Yes, intelligence, too: does that surprise you? I tell you, no one on earth, not even the greatest scientist or the greatest genius, is as intelligent as a ray of sunlight!

So concentrate on the sun's rays: long for them, seek them out, love and cherish them, open up your hearts to them, and you will begin to understand the meaning of creation; your own lives will become creative, meaningful and full of wonder and fulfilment. There are spiritual beings dwelling in each ray of sunshine and they manifest themselves differently according to the different colours: red, blue, green, yellow and so on. This is why it is so important for a disciple to learn to work with light.

Notes
1. See *Angels and other Mysteries of The Tree of Life,* Izvor Coll. n° 236, chap. 11: 'The body of Adam Kadmon'.
2. See *The Yoga of Nutrition,* Izvor Coll. n° 204, chap. 3: 'Food, a love-letter from God'.
3. See *Respiration – Spiritual Dimensions and Practical Applications,* Brochure n° 303.

Chapter Three

GOLD IS CONDENSED SUNLIGHT

When you find light it begins to produce tremendous changes in you, and the first of these is that it heightens your zest, your capacity for enjoyment. Whatever your activity, whatever you eat or drink, wherever you go, whatever you read, everything seems to take on a new, delicious flavour, an exquisite taste. But if you lose the light you find no enjoyment in anything any more, for in losing the light you have lost what is essential. *'If the salt loses its flavour... it is good for nothing but to be thrown out and trampled underfoot by men'*, said Jesus.[1] If you lose the light, the wheels of life will grind you to powder, because you will have lost your most powerful form of protection. Unfortunately you are well-informed about everything except the essentials. You know how to learn a trade, how to earn money, how to get yourself a good position in society, and your life is focused exclusively on these concerns; but have you ever been taught how to find light? Never!

If you don't work with light, if you don't understand what light is, it means that you don't understand the first thing about life itself. Light is everything! Light is the cause and origin of the universe. Light is a spirit, a spirit that emanates from the sun. Each ray of light is a potent force which penetrates and works on matter everywhere. If there is any one area which you should really study and concentrate on, it is light: what light is, how it works in the universe and how we, too, can work with it. He who neglects light on the grounds that he has got too much to do, that he must think about earning his living, and so forth, is on the wrong track.

If people are so fond of gold and always so eager to possess it, it is because, although they cannot remember it consciously, a secret knowledge about gold lies hidden in their subconscious: namely, that gold is a condensed, concentrated form of sunlight, and that that light contains life and power. They should try to understand, therefore, that rather than hunting for gold, they would do better to look for the light, because light is the head, whereas gold is only the tail. Light is the soul and the spirit and gold is the physical body. If you grasp the body without touching the soul, you have grasped nothing. If you have a body without a soul, all you have got is a cadaver. Besides, it is very dangerous to want to possess gold before you possess light. You know what happens to someone who catches hold of a snake by its tail: he gets bitten! You have to get hold of a snake by its head because when you do this, not only will you be quite safe, but you will have the tail too.

This is why I tell you to love light, to concentrate on light, for light is a symbol of God Himself. In this way you will receive some seeds of gold and with them you will be in a position to make mountains of gold for yourself. It is true! Look at sages and initiates: they possess quantities of gold. If you were clairvoyant, you would see that they were surrounded by countless particles and rays of gold. An initiate is surrounded by an aura of light, an aura of living gold, that which the alchemists called 'potable gold' because man can drink it; it is like a stream, a river. In the past, alchemists used to prescribe potions which contained gold and, even today, some tonics can be had in which there are salts of gold.

But that is not the best way to introduce gold into your bodies. It can do you some good, of course, but not enough. Gold has to be eaten, drunk and imbibed inwardly in the form of ideas and thoughts: the very best, most luminous ideas and thoughts. If you do this then, yes, you will obtain true gold. Unfortunately this is not what most human beings do; all they think about is getting

rich at all costs just as quickly as possible, and the
result is that gold becomes a screen between
themselves and their fellow men. They see other
people as obstacles to be overcome, rivals to be
eliminated, and they become cruel and hard-
hearted. Their minds are so obsessed by gold that
it becomes a screen which obscures their vision for
anything else. Anyone whose mind is infatuated by
gold is bound to be influenced in this way. Perhaps
you will say, 'Well, if I'm not to fill my mind with
gold, what should I do with it? Where can I put it?'
Fill your pockets with it, if you like; pile it up in
your safe, put it wherever you like except in your
head: never in your head! By which I mean don't
keep thinking about it, don't yearn for it, don't look
for it. The only thing you should put in your head
is light, wisdom. If you do that then you will
possess gold, true gold.

Several years ago I knew a man who was so
obsessed by a desire for gold that he ended by
practising magic in the hope of conjuring up nature
spirits and getting them to show him the secret
places where gold and treasure was hidden. Night
and day he thought of nothing but that: gold and
hidden treasure. So one day I said to him: 'Listen,
you are a guest in a palace and instead of showering
all your love and attention on the princess, you
spend your time flirting with her maid. She's the
one you smile and wink at; she's the one whose

hand you kiss. You're not behaving very intelligently!' He could only look at me in astonishment, so I explained further: 'Yes, you see, you are in the royal palace of the universe and instead of becoming intimate with the princess (light) who could give you everything your heart desires, open all doors to you and shower you with all the treasures of her palace, you waste your time trying to ingratiate yourself with a common maid-servant (gold) who has no influence and no power. You spend all your time looking for earthly gold, instead of looking for the celestial gold which you can find in the sun and which is light. From now on you must try to get to know light, for light is the princess. Think of her often, talk to her, give her a lot of love and, in the long run it is she who will order gold to come to you too. Since it was light that produced gold she has authority over it. But as long as you have not established a solid bond of love with light, she will never order gold to put itself at your service. She will say, "You should pay homage to me, first of all; you should be courting me. But you are neglecting me and running after the chambermaid. Very well, if that's how it is, you will find all the doors closed in your face!" ' 'Ah,' said my friend; 'Now I understand.' But I'm afraid he had not really understood at all, because he is still looking for gold—which he never finds, incidentally, and it is just as well, for if he

did, he would become really terrible! Ah, yes!
More often than not that is what gold – money –
does: it makes people cruel, vicious and mean.
Whereas spiritual gold, on the contrary, opens their
hearts and gives them a broad, limitless view of life
and the beauties of nature.

Perhaps you will object: 'But people who have
lots of gold, lots of money, are influential; they can
have whatever they want!' Yes, they can have some
bric-a-brac, some shadows, some smoke. And then,
after a while, they realize that not only have they
really got nothing at all, but they have lost their
health, their peace of mind and all their friends into
the bargain. Only those who have understood that
light is the only true gold, will obtain everything:
knowledge, love and happiness and, in addition, all
the gold they want.

True! If you have got a lot of money it will
open the doors of the material, physical world for
you, but the other doors, the doors of peace,
happiness, joy and inspiration, the doors of all the
qualities and virtues will remain closed to you.
What is the point of having all the doors to the
material world open if the doors of the inner
sanctuary remain closed? You will eat, work and
go about your business without any sense of
pleasure, without enjoyment: the spiritual doors
are closed to you – and all because your
understanding of life and its values is false.

You must pay homage and give all your love to the princess, for then all her retainers will be at your service. The princess only has to say the word: 'Bring him food and drink; give him fine raiment; get a room ready for him,' and her servants will hasten to obey: 'At once, Your Highness. Certainly Princess!' And when you go out for a stroll with the princess, all her courtiers will be there to accompany you and make themselves agreeable to you.

If you prefer gold to the light, it will dazzle you and you will be unable to see anything else. Once the notion of gold – money – has taken hold of your heart and mind you are lost: you will have no eyes for anything else, not even the beauty, splendour and intelligence of creation. You will exclaim, 'But what's he talking about? You have to have money; you can't get along without it!' How well I know it! I am not denying that money is a necessity. What I am saying is that you must not enthrone money in your mind and make it your ideal, your master, your goal in life. Money can be a means, an instrument, an occasion, yes; but it must be at the service of an ideal and that ideal must be the light; light must be your goal in life. Never let money become your master; it can be a wonderful servant but it is a very bad master, and it would give you the most appalling advice which would cause you to abandon the kingdom of God.

So think about light, because it is light that brings wealth (not money: wealth); it is light that brings spiritual power; it is light that brings true enjoyment. When you possess light you find that you take pleasure in the least little things: a glass of fresh water tastes as delicious as the elixir of eternal life and quenches your thirst as though the water were actually coursing through your veins. It is an indescribable feeling!

Hermes Trismegistus, Master of the Mysteries, said, 'The father thereof is the sun, the mother the moon. The wind carried it in its womb, the earth is the nurse thereof.' The four elements were there: the sun (fire), the moon (water), the wind (air) and the earth. The four elements collaborated to bring to birth and nurture that light, that quintessence which Hermes Trismegistus calls telesma and which confers all knowledge and all powers on initiates.[2]

Tradition tells us, also, that Zarathustra once asked the god Ahura-Mazda what the first man ate, and Ahura-mazda replied, 'He ate fire and drank light.' Why should we not learn, also, to eat fire and drink light and so be restored to the primeval perfection of the first man?

Learn to find nourishment in light, for in doing so you will find the greatest possible blessings; you will feel so rich that you will begin to love every

creature that exists. It is poverty that engenders
hatred. The rich never hate anyone. But be sure,
now, that you understand me correctly: I am talking
of the truly rich, the great masters. They live in
such abundance that their hearts overflow; how
could they possibly harbour feelings of hatred
when they enjoy such plenitude? It is those who
feel deprived who are aggressive and envious and
detest other people. When you see someone who
does not like others, who manifests no inner nobility or generosity, you can be sure that he feels poor
and wretched in himself.

Never forget this. As soon as someone becomes
conscious of the wealth that God bestows on him
so lavishly, his heart overflows with love and his
one thought is to help and enlighten others. Being
in possession of such superabundance he is
impelled to share it with others. Whereas he who
feels his poverty is envious of the rich, so he attacks
and robs them. This explains why poverty – poverty
in all its forms – is the root cause of crime.

Blessed are those who have enthroned light,
spiritual light, in the sanctuary of their minds,
souls, hearts and spirits, for this is true wealth.
Perhaps some of you may ask, 'But how can one
obtain this inner light?' What a question! Don't
you know how primitives set about making fire?
They rub two pieces of wood together until they
produce heat; then they go on rubbing and even-

tually a tiny flame blazes up and gives light. As you see, there are three stages to the process: first, movement (the will), second, heat (love, feeling) and third, light (intelligence, thought).

So if you want to obtain light you must make up your minds to act, set your will to work until heat, love, takes hold of you and keep working until that love, in turn, becomes light. That is how to obtain light! Practise spiritual exercises, meditation and prayer until you find so much enjoyment in them that you cannot do without them any longer and, eventually, light will blaze up. Of course you can follow the reverse movement, also: you can convert light into heat and heat into movement. Certain elements of knowledge in the intellect can give rise to love in the heart, and that love urges you to act. So it is a two-way process. It is all so simple! People stagnate for years, puzzling over how to obtain light, how to live a spiritual life, and never managing to do so... and yet it is all so simple!

Notes

1. See *The Philosopher's Stone – in the Gospels and in Alchemy,* Izvor Coll. n° 241, chap. 3: 'You are the salt of the earth', and chap. 4: 'But if the salt loses its flavour...', chap. 6: 'You are the light of the world'.
2. Op. cit., chap. 9: 'The work of the alchemist: 3 over 4' and chap. 14: 'The gold of true knowledge: the alchemist and the gold prospector'.

Chapter Four

LIGHT ENABLES US TO SEE AND BE SEEN

The essential quality of light is that it allows us to see: thanks to light we can see not only the dangers but also the blessings along the path we tread. Light reveals reality to us. Everything that exists has its own particular properties and light alone has the property of enlightening us and showing us the way. Suppose you have gone for a walk in the dark, you cannot see where you are, but you switch on your torch and it reveals that you are on the edge of a cliff! 'Two steps more,' you exclaim; 'and that would have been the end of me!'

Everything has its own particular properties. Light, of course, cannot fill your stomach, nor your purse! But it might show you where some treasure has been buried, and then you can go and dig it up and become very rich. Whereas, if you have a lot of money but no light, a thief will be sure to come and rob you, because those who have no light are an easy prey for thieves. This is true in the inner life as well as in the outer life. In fact, this is what Jesus was referring to when he said: *'Lay up for your-selves treasures in heaven, where neither moth nor rust destroys and where thieves do not break in and steal.'*[1] This parable has been with us for the last two thousand years and yet no one has ever interpreted it correctly, because no one has ever understood that thieves, moth and rust represent dangers which threaten man in his three essential faculties: the intellect, the heart and the will.

Yes, thieves and robbers who take advantage of the dark to do their sinister work unseen, symbolize the dangers threatening the intellect when it has lost its light. As soon as man loses the light, thieves – that is to say, all kinds of extravagant ideas, doubts and worries – insinuate themselves into his mind, leaving him impoverished and weak and even leading, sometimes, to insanity. Psychiatric hospitals are full of people who had extinguished the light of their minds and been broken into and robbed of everything they possessed by thieves who took advantage of their darkness. If you want to protect yourselves, therefore, light your lamps. Why do you think that shop windows are lit up at night? Because light is a protection.

One day I was talking to some police officers, and I asked them: 'Do you really think that you could fight crime more successfully if you had more policemen and detectives and better security methods? If so you are mistaken; external methods

are totally ineffectual in this area. The only effective means of action is light!' They looked at me in
astonishment: 'Light? How can light...?' 'Think
about it,' I replied; 'If crooks know that they can
break the law and plan all kinds of robberies, hold-
ups, kidnappings and murders, it is because they
know that, in most cases, people don't suspect
anything; they have no intuition to warn them to
take the necessary precautions. But imagine what
would happen if people had an inner light which
warned them in advance and at a distance if
someone were plotting to do them an injury: they
would take precautions against it and the evil plan
would miscarry. So the only possible method for
wiping out crime is light. This is why human beings
have to be taught how to increase their inner light.
It is something that will take a long time; no doubt
about that; but it is the only sure way.' Naturally,
the police officers looked at me in utter amazement:
they had never thought of anything like that.

Until such time as human beings have learned
to develop that inner light which is the only
possible means by which to see and foresee, they
are bound to be taken in, at some time or another,
by those who concentrate all their energies on
hatching and perpetrating their villainies. Even the
most sophisticated technical devices will not
protect you against criminals, because they know
how to use them, too. Think of all the bank

robberies we hear about: in spite of armour-plated strong-rooms and electronic alarm systems, the thieves achieve their ends because they are just as well equipped. All the technical improvements used by the police can equally be used by gangsters. Crime will never be wiped out until people make up their minds to use light.

If we are able to see, it is because rays of light fall on objects and make them visible to us. Without light we cannot see anything; and this shows that if there is a world which remains invisible to us, it is simply because we are incapable of casting light onto the objects and entities of that world. Whereas, if the initiates, by contrast, are able to see so much that is invisible to others, it is because they know how to project rays of light.

These are truths which men know nothing about. Besides, where will you find people who are ready to teach others how to project light from their hearts and minds, from their souls and spirits? It is so much more interesting to teach them how to get on in society, how to make a lot of money or get a good job! The trouble is, though, that however much they 'get on', it doesn't prevent them from being ill and unhappy. This is why people must learn to work with light, only with light, and learn to project that light which alone enables us to see. Ah, yes! Have you never wondered why nothing else in the whole world, however valuable, such as gold or precious stones, has the power to dispel darkness? How can you explain that the Creator has given this extraordinary power to light alone?

If you understand the language of symbols, you will understand that 'darkness' means all forms of suffering, weakness and illness, and that only light is empowered to combat them effectively. It is no use looking for other ways of remedying your problems. Anyone who has got to go down into a cellar or a dark cave, knows that he must light a lamp, a physical light; but when it comes to their own inner lives it never occurs to people to use light.

In fact, I shall go even further: the light which enables us to see, also enables us to be seen. The world is like an ocean on a dark night, and you are like so many tiny boats, drifting rudderless on the face of that ocean; if you want to be found and rescued by exalted entities who are somewhere above you, ready to help, you must send up flares of light so that they can see where you are. If you are a speck of darkness in the midst of darkness, how can you expect them to find you? Jesus told his disciples to *'pray'*,[2] and to pray means to send out powerful vibrations, and in the eyes of heaven there is no power greater than that of light. Heaven is not drawn to that which has no light; if you want Heaven to take care of you, you are going to have to light all your lamps.

Do you really want the divine world to answer all those questions that torment you? Well, if your questions are always accompanied by signals of light, then you can be sure of getting an answer. But I warn you that if you ask your questions in any other way you will not get an answer. Heaven never gives in to any other inducement: light is the only thing that has the power to persuade heaven.

Notes
1. See *New Light on the Gospels,* Izvor Coll. n° 217, chap. 4: 'Lay up for yourselves treasures in heaven'.
2. See *The True Meaning of Christ's Teaching,* Izvor Coll. n° 215, chap. 9: 'Watch and pray', and *La prière,* Brochure n° 305.

Chapter Five

WORKING WITH LIGHT

There are a great many people in the world who yearn to receive divine revelations and experience the thrill of inspiration and ecstasy, but they have the impression that all that is extremely difficult to achieve. In point of fact, it is very simple, so simple that if I were to tell them how to set about it they would not believe me. The result is that they will never do anything to obtain these things, so they will never know the splendours of the divine world.

Many years ago, when I was still a very young disciple of the Master Peter Deunov, I asked him, 'What is the best way to be close to God and to develop my spiritual faculties and virtues?' And he told me, 'You must think constantly of light, concentrate on it, picture the whole universe bathed in light.' Well, I worked with this image of light for a very long time and learned a great deal from it. In reality, God is not light; He is far more than that. One cannot know or even imagine God. And if the

Book of Genesis says that, on the first day, God created light, this means that He, Himself, is not light but that He created the universe out of light.

God is not light, but since light is the first divine emanation, it contains all the qualities and virtues of God, and one can know God only through light.[1] So, now let me give you an exercise to do every day, several times a day: as soon as you have a few spare minutes concentrate your thought on light, rest in light, melt into light, soak yourself in light and picture the whole universe bathed in that light. Little by little, as you do this, you will find that all the elements of your being begin to fall into place, that this light is bringing you true knowledge, lasting peace, inner balance and power. Instead of wasting your time on all kinds of useless activities, use it to think of the light that illuminates and gives life and peace.

You will never find the true meaning of life anywhere but in light. Let's take just one very simple example from everyday life: when you wake up in the middle of the night and want to get up, the very first thing you do is switch on a light. As long as you can see, you can do whatever you want, but if you try to move about in the dark you will bump into things and knock them over and hurt yourself. Well, the strange thing is that people have never understood what this teaches us about light: they continue to move about and work in the dark – symbolically speaking; they can't see where they are and so they are constantly 'bumping into things.'

You must seek the light; you must concentrate on it, eat and drink it, attach more importance to it than to all the other precious things on earth. As soon as you have a free moment, close your eyes and fix your mind on the image of that light which pervades all things and is the source of all blessings. While you are waiting for a train, or in the dentist's waiting room, instead of reading all the rubbish you find in magazines, spend a few minutes thinking of light.

If you are out in the street, for instance, and you find yourself assailed by negative feelings or thoughts, obviously, you cannot stop and close your eyes (otherwise there would be a crowd round you in no time at all; people would even bring their chairs and sit and watch you, and you would be arrested for obstructing the traffic!). But there is nothing to prevent you from stopping in front of a shop window as though you wanted to look at the goods on display and, as long as no one can see you from the inside, concentrating for a few moments while you try to light your inner lamps. After a few moments you can go on your way, refreshed and purified.

Most human beings have no notion of these methods; they will plod along for an hour or more, or even for the rest of the day, their minds weighed down with problems fit to kill them. It never occurs to them to stop in a park, for instance, and try to change their negative vibrations by communing with the trees, flowers or fountains. Oh, no; they would rather go and have a drink at a pub and watch people coming and going (for all the world like cows watching the trains go by), after which they go on their way again, still carrying their sorry burdens. And in the evening they take them home and pass them on to their wives: 'Hello, darling!' And with one quick kiss they deposit all their gloom on her. And she, in turn, passes it on to the children – and so it goes! This is how people live: stupidly and unconsciously.

Even though I am talking to you like this, I am not at all sure that any of you will be interested in doing this work of concentrating on light and seeing what effect it has on you, how it can model, purify, vivify and resuscitate you. People are always ready to open their doors and their hearts to things that can only entail complications and problems, but they never seem to have any time or any room in their lives for light. And this is why human beings are permanently weak and miserable: because they have not opened their minds, hearts, souls and spirits to the only thing that is worthwhile: light.

The exercise I have just given you can be applied in all circumstances: if you are cooking, writing letters, washing, dressing or undressing, you can always find a few seconds in which to picture in your mind the light that bathes the whole universe. Many clairvoyants have actually seen that light: they have seen that all creatures, all objects down to the very stones of the earth are not only bathed in light, they emanate light.

To begin with, this light was known as 'astral light', because it was like the light of the stars. But above and beyond this, there is another, subtler light. Perhaps, sometimes, when you have been meditating or are in a particularly spiritual frame of mind, you have been lit up from within as though by some inner sun, as though a thousands lamps suddenly glowed within you, and you have even sensed that that light shone out from your face. Once you reach the higher levels of kindness and generosity, gentleness and purity, you will be irradiated with light, you can actually see it; everything becomes clearer and more luminous. Whereas if you indulge in feelings of jealousy, selfishness and greed, you don't need a mirror to tell you what your face reveals: you can sense the darkness in it.

Now, of course, you must be careful not to generalize. When you see a shadow on someone's face, you must not immediately conclude that he is moved by evil thoughts or evil intentions. No, if you have no other elements with which to form a judgment you will probably be mistaken: it could be, for instance, that someone else is throwing their shadow onto that person's face. He, himself, is not in darkness, but a cloud or some other object is casting a shadow. And similarly, when you see light shining from a person's face, it may simply mean that someone else is playing with mirrors, and those mirrors are reflecting light onto his face. It is not the person himself who has created such light; some entity has been there, briefly, playing with light, and when it has gone, the light goes too. If you want to be able to form a judgment about someone based on what you see in his face, you must be capable of seeing beyond appearances. But there is one thing you can be sure of, and that is that the light within you varies in accordance with your thoughts and feelings, your hopes, desires and intentions.

The truth is that love has an extremely important role to play in obtaining this inner light: it is important that you understand this correctly. When you understand what love really is and how to manifest it, how to let it flow through you, then you will become luminous. Perhaps you will tell me that you don't see the connection. Well, that is what I am going to show you.

You all know how primitives produced fire: they would take two bits of wood, for example, and rub them together until the friction produced heat, and the heat produced a flame. So there are three stages: movement, heat and light. And now, if you interpret this phenomenon you will see that movement corresponds to the activity produced by the will; heat corresponds to the feelings produced by the heart, and the flame, the light, corresponds to thought which is the fruit of the intellect. As far as love is concerned, one could say that, symbolically speaking, human beings never get beyond the stage of movement. True, this movement does produce warmth, but they must rise far beyond this purely sensory satisfaction, all the way to the light, to understanding, to the heart of the mysteries of the universe. Yes, love can lead men to this goal, but only if they cease to think of it as no more than an agreeable effervescence. There is a whole body of science which a disciple can study in order to learn to produce light, but pleasure must no longer be his sole interest, for pleasure absorbs all one's energies and prevents the light from shining.[2]

When we are together and meditate in silence, put all your cares to one side and concentrate on light as though everything depended on it, as though your very life depended on it. Think of it as though you were living your last moments, you are about to leave the world and light is the only thing that can save you: cling to it. Light! Nothing else matters. This is the most marvellous of exercises.

You can picture a white, incandescent light, and join your voice to that of the initiates as they declare: 'I am a fragment of fragments of the incandescent Soul.' Or you can picture it as purple, blue, green, yellow, orange or red; but it is preferable to picture white light, for white light combines and unites all the others. White light can give you the omnipotence of purple, the peace and truth of blue, the wealth and eternal youth of green, the wisdom and knowledge of yellow, the health, vigour and vitality of orange, the activity and dynamic energy of red. But, above all, picture white light to yourself. When you reach the stage of concentrating completely on light, when you sense it as a vibrant, throbbing, quivering ocean of peace, happiness and joy, then you will also begin to sense it as perfume and as music, that cosmic music which we call the music of the spheres, the song of the whole universe.

There is no more worthy, more glorious or more potent work than this work with light. If you really want to devote yourself to something truly great and noble, this is it; there is none other. Every other activity has both a good and bad side to it. If you are honestly observant about yourself, you will have to recognize that, whatever your profession, after a few years it has taken its toll, it has cost you your strength, health and beauty. Obviously it will also have brought you some good things: money, probably, and perhaps a little fame or recognition; but if you weigh that in the divine balance you will be forced to admit that the little you have gained in no way compensates for all the riches you have lost.

Unfortunately, human beings are not in the habit of weighing things up in this manner. They do all kinds of other calculations perhaps, but when they want money, honours, fame or knowledge they never weigh them up against all the losses involved: their peace, health, joy and purity. They often manage to get what they set their hearts on, but a few years later they find themselves in hospital or in a psychiatric clinic, unable even to eat and drink and enjoy themselves normally. When this happens they begin to realize the value of what they have lost. 'Ah, if I'd only known...,' they say, sadly. But by then it is too late. They should have known before. So, you, who *do* know, be sure to devote more and more time to thinking about light. It is the only activity that can really make you rich and healthy. Believe me, every other activity, even those which bring you a few little advantages, robs you of so many other, far more precious things. Cast your mind back over your past life and you will see how true this is.

From now on, therefore, whenever you feel the urge to launch into an occupation designed to bring you more worldly advantages, take the time to think about this, and weigh up what it will cost you in at least two other areas: your health and your spiritual evolution. My task is to give you the criteria which you can then apply in order to transform your lives, to enter, in other words, into the new life. If I had to try and please you by preaching the rules for the old life, it would not be worth it: I might as well close up shop at once! So, I shall go on teaching you the great laws which can help men to live more wisely and find the way back to their heavenly homeland. The fact that there may be very few who want to abide by these laws is irrelevant: my job is to go on giving them to you.

Henceforth, whether you are here, together with many others, or all alone at home; wherever you may be, remember to make contact with that source of all blessings: light, nothing but light.

Many years ago (I must have been about twenty at the time), I read a passage from the *Zohar* which I have never forgotten. It was in Bulgarian, of course, but let me translate it for you: *'Seven lights there are in the Highest of Heights, and therein dwells the Ancient of Ancients, the Hidden of all the Hidden Ones, the Secret of all Secrets, Ain Soph.'* When I recited these words everything within me started to vibrate and quiver.

Those seven lights are the seven colours, and each one corresponds to a particular virtue or quality: purple corresponds to sacrifice, blue to truth, green to hope, yellow to wisdom, orange to sanctity and red to love. But you must realize that with every fault that man commits, the power which corresponds to one of these colours diminishes. It is almost useless, therefore, to work with light and colour in the hope of acquiring spiritual powers if you don't sustain and support these powers by practising the corresponding virtues. Anyone who thinks that he can become a great magus simply by performing certain rites and practices without making any improvements in his inner life is greatly mistaken. Attempts of that kind will never enlist the cooperation of higher entities; the only creatures who will respond will be from the lowest levels, elementals and monsters. If your goal is to attract angels and archangels, you must know that you can do so only by your virtues; the higher entities respond only to those who are capable of manifesting true light, that is to say, purity, love, wisdom and truth.

You must also realize that the only means that is permissible in attempting to win someone's friendship and affection, is that of light. Everybody uses money, seduction, violence or expensive gifts, because they think that these are the most effective means. But the only means acceptable to Heaven (and which is also the most powerful) is light. So if you want someone to think of you and love you, send him a gift of spiritual light, a bouquet of light; surround him with light. If you do this, his soul, feeling the presence of a beneficial entity, will appreciate you more and more.

Do you want your friends to be pleased to see you when you go to visit them? If so, don't make the mistake of most people, and go to see them when you are feeling depressed, irritable or worried. Before you go into someone's house, stop and recollect yourself for a few moments and picture that house and all who live in it bathed in light. If you do this how could they be anything but pleased to see you?

Light must be your constant preoccupation. Wherever you may be, as soon as you have a moment's respite: think of light. When you feel that grief, difficulty or doubt is casting a shadow over your soul: go and talk to the light about it. Say, 'Oh, Light, you who are the most intelligent of beings, enter my heart and mind and shine in them.' And the light will come and make everything bright and clear. If you want to help someone who is in difficulty, send him rays of light, imagine him being penetrated through and through by those rays. And if you, yourself, have a pain, imagine rays of light of different colours streaming from your fingers to the painful spot, and before long you will feel the pain easing.

Know that you will be really fit and well only when you have learned to surround yourself with a strong, pure aura containing all the colours of the spectrum. This is the only true medicine. A powerful aura is the best form of protection; it acts as a barrier to shield you from all negative currents and anything that could distress you. To have a strong aura like that is to be in a fortress; when others all around are ill, alarmed and distressed, a man with a strong aura is never discouraged, never loses his love, because he feels the luminous presence which dwells in him and makes him capable of helping others.

Try to understand the importance of this work with light, and you will have an infallible instrument at your disposal. If you don't get results as fast as you would like, it is because you have been estranged from light for too long. You have collected so many dense, opaque elements, that light cannot get through, your 'walls' are too thick; but you can help the light to break through by purifying yourself so that your walls become thinner and more transparent.[3]

One day, at long last, light will blaze forth and flood all things; then the Universal White Brotherhood will triumph throughout the world. But bright, shining, living lamps are needed, lamps such as the Rabbi Simeon ben Yohai who was known as 'The

Holy Lamp' because he cast light all around him; and when he died it was said that the lamp had gone out. But that lamp still shines in the other world!

Notes

1. See *The Fruits of The Tree of Life – The Cabbalistic Tradition,* Complete Works, vol. 32, chap. 5: 'The creation of the world and the theory of emanation'.

2. See *Love and Sexuality,* Complete Works, vol. 14, chap. 9: 'From Yesod to Kether: the path of sexual sublimation', and vol. 15, chap. 4: 'The goal of love is light'.

3. See *Looking into the Invisible – Intuition, Clairvoyance, Dreams,* Izvor Coll. n° 228, chap. 3: 'The entrance to the invisible world: from Yesod to Tiphareth'.

Chapter Six

THE PRISM: A SYMBOL OF MAN

The prism shows that white light can be split up into seven different colours.

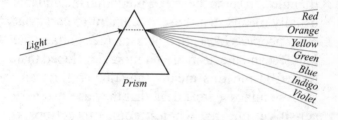

This phenomenon by which white light is decomposed is based on three significant numbers: 1, 3 and 7. The 1 represents the ray of light that strikes the surface of the prism; the 3 represents the prism itself, with its three sides, and the 7 represents the colours diffracted by the prism.

A symbolical parallel can be drawn between the three sides of a prism and the three faculties which govern the actions of a human being: intellect, heart and will. If the human prism is to diffract and radiate the seven colours harmoniously, he has to be transparent and equilateral, which means that his heart, intellect and will must be equally developed. He must have a kind heart and a good mind and be capable of putting his thoughts and feelings into effect. If this is the case, then everything within him will be harmonious. But, as we all know, such cases are very rare. In fact we could say that the equilateral prism represents the initiate, the sage, the great master.

More often than not, people represent lopsided triangles. In some the will is predominant, and this usually means that they are content to carry out other people's ideas. In others, on the contrary, the intellect and the heart are far more developed than the will, and this means that they reflect and analyse things a great deal, that they are also very sensitive, but that when it comes to action, to getting things done, they wait for others to act for them. And so on and so forth: there are all kinds of different cases. The essential thing to understand, however, is that we must all do our very best to become equilateral triangles so as to be capable of radiating the seven colours, that is to say, the seven virtues.

We have no need to create light: it is already there, ready and waiting to pass through us and do its work in us. It is we who are not ready; it is we who are neither properly developed nor sufficiently pure. Yes, God is willing and ready to enter each human being and to manifest Himself within him in all the splendour of the seven rays of light, that is to say, to give him all possible virtues and powers, but man is so drab, lopsided and under-developed, that God can only manifest Himself very imperfectly through him.

The first thing to do, therefore, is to restore balance within oneself. If, up to date, you have developed primarily your intellect, for example, you must now find ways of developing your heart; later you will have to work and make the effort to develop your will. When the triangle of heart, mind and will is perfectly developed in a man, he finds that light automatically penetrates his being and radiates from him in the form of the seven colours.[1]

And now, let's look at the different functions of the human body in relation to what we have been saying: each one of them reproduces the pheno-menon of the prism which decomposes white light into seven colours. When you eat, for instance, the food represents white light, the prism is represented by your stomach, and it must be in good condition to digest the food and distribute the seven forces, the seven colours, to the rest of the body. The red is sent to the muscles, the orange to the circulatory system, the yellow to the nervous system, the green to the digestive system, the blue to the respiratory system, the indigo to the skeleton and the purple to the endocrine glands and the chakras.

The same pattern can be seen with the air we breathe: the air symbolizes the light of the sun and the respiratory organs (nose and lungs, whose role parallels that of the stomach), represent the prism. The blood, purified and oxygenated in the lungs, distributes the seven rays of energy throughout the body.

The same phenomenon can be seen even with our organs of sight and hearing: just as light enters a prism, images and sounds enter our eyes and ears and are diffracted and relayed to us in the form of impressions. Every single thing that enters into man, therefore, whatever he absorbs or perceives, can be compared to the beam of light which enters a prism on one side and emerges from the other side in the form of seven rays. The process is the same in every instance.

And now let's look at the question of quantities: when the stomach distributes the energy it has extracted from its food, it sends four parts to the digestive and sexual organs, two parts to the heart and lungs and only one part to the brain. The explanation for this is to be found in another division known to esoterics and which is traditional in initiatic science: that of head, thorax and belly. The head corresponds to the divine world, the world of intelligence; the thorax (heart and lungs) corresponds to the astral world, and the belly (digestive and sexual organs) corresponds to the physical world. The stomach absorbs food and distributes it to the body, keeping four parts for its own region and sending two parts to the heart and lungs and one to the brain. The lungs keep three parts of the air they absorb for themselves and the heart, send two parts to the belly and two to the brain. And, finally, when the brain receives energy from the sun, it keeps four parts for itself and sends two to the heart and lungs and only one to the belly. Only a very small proportion of the spiritual elements, which leave very little waste, are present in the stomach; it is the nervous system that receives by far the greatest share. Almost all the energies received from food and drink, on the other hand, go into the muscular system and digestive systems; very little goes to the brain.

What is essential, here, is to understand the message of the prism which teaches us to work on ourselves until we are as pure as a crystal, and to develop the three dimensions of head, lungs and belly until they form a harmonious triangle. When we achieve this, the light in which we are immersed will enter and pass through us, emerging in the form of seven rays of beautiful, shimmering colours.

I have already spoken to you about the symbolism of the two triangles: the one pointing upwards and the other pointing down. Some of you already know that these two equilateral triangles are symbols of men and women who have developed their heart, intellect and will to the point of perfection.

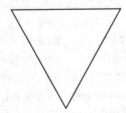 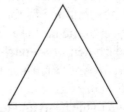

The triangle of man points down, because it represents the cosmic Spirit which comes down to earth and penetrates into matter, to vivify and spiritualize it and give it some of its own energy; this is the triangle of involution. The triangle of woman points upwards because it symbolizes matter which looks up to her beloved, the spirit: this is evolution. Each of them goes half-way and when they meet, embrace and fuse into one, both find perfect fulfilment. This union of spirit and matter is symbolized by the hexagram or seal of Solomon.

When a man and woman become one in order to create a child, the man gives light, the 1, to the

woman, and she, who represents the 3, produces the 7, the seven rays of force: a complete human being. It is still the same law that is operative here. If the woman is not 'symmetrical' she cannot produce a perfect spectrum of colours, that is to say, she cannot produce a whole human being, endowed with all its members and a full range of faculties and qualities: she will produce a cripple. The nature of the child depends, therefore, on the mother; but it depends on the father, too, for what he gives her is not always as pure and luminous as the light of the sun. We can be sure of one thing: he gives the woman light of a kind, whether brilliant or pale, and this light passes through the imperfect prism of the mother who produces a child, and the child reflects the imperfections of its parents. The correspondences with the phenomenon of the prism are absolute![2]

In fact, when I talk to you, my words are like sunlight and you yourselves are so many prisms. If

my words are as pure, intelligent and perfect as the
light of the sun, and if you are properly propor-
tioned prisms, by which I mean if you are well
rested, attentive and wide awake, and if your minds
and hearts are well disposed, marvellous children
in the form of ideas, enthusiasm and constructive
decisions will be born. But if you are drowsy and
tired and indifferent to my words you cannot be
good prisms and then, even if I revealed the greatest
and most profound truths to you the results would
not amount to anything; in fact all kinds of
misunderstandings would probably arise because
you would put a wrong interpretation on my
words.

And now, let me reveal something else which
is very interesting: an initiate who possesses both
triangles, the masculine and feminine principles, in
himself, represents the union of spirit and matter.
When he is filled with kindness, love and
compassion for men and intent on obtaining every
kind of blessing for them, he represents the triangle
of the spirit, that which points down, towards
humanity. Then he receives a ray of divine light
from God and, although all his activity is aimed
downwards, towards men, yet that light is diffracted
and radiates from him in a beam of seven colours
that reaches all the way to heaven, and all the
angels and archangels and even the Almighty
marvel at the beauty of it.

The feminine principle on the other hand, that which is symbolized by the triangle pointing upwards, is much closer to the centre of the earth, and the centre of the earth also projects a beam of light, but it is a dark light, an infernal light, which can have a devastating effect on those who are not pure, intelligent and vigilant. So, as I have just said, when an initiate has a totally selfless love for mankind, and when his whole soul and all his strength are concentrated in a prayer for all men, that they may know joy, peace, abundance and fulfilment, the seven rays of colour shine from him. And, at this point, something very important happens: all the hostile, dark forces projected onto the initiate from hell, are purified and transformed by him and used to further his own work. For a great initiate there is no evil that cannot be transformed into light and joy.[3] It is only when man is not closely bound to divine light and has not developed his intelligence and his will, that dark, subterranean influences can perturb him and even cause his fall.

The brain, lungs and stomach all diffuse seven forces throughout the human body: $3 \times 7 = 21$, and if you add man himself to this number, you have 22. The 22 keys, the 22 arcana of the tarot. Or, if you prefer not to add man because you consider that he is already included in the 21 forces, you can replace him by light, the light that gives birth to all these forces. So we have seven energies for the head, seven for the heart and lungs and seven for the belly, and with the light of the sun, this gives twenty-two.

The whole of life, the multitude of affinities and correspondences that make up life, is represented by this image of the prism which breaks up white light into the seven colours. And this is why I am now giving you this rule: seek the light, imagine that you are a prism and that you are so well orientated that you take the white light that enters you and send it out in all directions as rays of seven glorious colours.

Notes

1. See *The Symbolic Language of Geometrical Figures,* Izvor Coll. n° 218, chap. 3: 'The triangle'.
2. See *Hope for the World: Spiritual Galvanoplasty,* Izvor Coll. n° 214, chap. 7: 'Love's goal is light', chap. 8: 'The solar nature of sexual energy', chap. 9: 'Mankind transformed'.
3 See *The Wellsprings of Eternal Joy,* Izvor Coll. n° 242.

Chapter Seven

PURITY CLEARS THE WAY FOR LIGHT

I

Every night, when men go to sleep, their souls go out from their physical bodies and plunge back into the universal Soul. While the body is resting, a considerable work of purification and cleansing goes on, and once it is done, the soul can return and take up its functions again, and manifest itself in matter in a variety of ways. This process repeats itself every night and even, for some people, during the day. At night, therefore, the soul goes out from the body (although it remains attached to it by the subtle bond known as the silver cord) and when it comes back in the morning, it finds its house swept, cleaned, and washed and it can take up its work where it left off. If the soul did not leave the body, men would be asphyxiated and die of poisoning, for the necessary cleaning process could not take place.

It is important to understand that life is combustion: the physical, emotional and mental activity which we refer to as 'life' produces energies, but it also produces wastes, and it takes time for these waste products to be eliminated. This is why the soul has to leave the body, so that it can be cleansed. And since it is because of the impurities in the physical body that the soul is obliged to leave it, it follows that the purer and more transparent a man is, the less his soul is obliged to leave his body. Obviously, when someone has overloaded his system with heavy, indigestible food (I am not talking only about physical food, but also about astral and mental food), the cleansing process takes a long time and the soul is obliged to prolong its absence. This is all quite easy to understand: when the cleaning woman bustles in with mops and pails and dusters, the master of the house has to leave his study and go somewhere else while she is cleaning it. In the same way, the soul is driven out of the body so that the cleaners can do their work.

The question now arises as to whether a person's soul necessarily rises to unite itself with the universal Soul, or whether it drifts about on a lower level. This all depends on the person and on the nature of his desires, thoughts and feelings, but at the moment I am talking about someone who is animated by a high spiritual ideal. During his sleep, the soul of such a person rises towards the light; it steeps itself in light, contemplates immensity, travels through space and communes with heavenly entities. And when it returns to its physical body it brings back with it memories of what it has experienced and tries to impress them on the brain. Even if the person is not immediately aware of this, he receives these indelible imprints and, sooner or later, they will all be revealed to him.[1]

This explains those sudden flashes of perception that sometimes come to you; they are manifestations of sublime truths that your subconscious has most certainly been treasuring for a long time. The time was not ripe for you to be aware of them sooner, and then a moment came when your brain was well disposed and, all of a sudden, the light flashed before your eyes. Of course, if you are already used to working with your physical body to purify it and render it more sensitive, your soul will be able to record the realities of the sublime world and communicate them to your conscious mind much more easily. This is why it is important to give your physical body pure food and drink, pure air and even pure thoughts, feelings and activities.

Spirituality does not consist in neglecting the material dimension and attaching importance only to the spirit, because the spirit can be greatly hampered in its manifestations by a poor degree of evolution of the physical body. The spirit is all-powerful; yes, but it cannot manifest its powers if the corresponding organs of our bodies have not been awakened. Alchemists understood this, and this is why they spent their time transforming, purifying and sublimating matter. All their work with metals in their crucibles, stills and athanors was symbolic. What they were really doing was working with water, air and fire, on their own physical bodies, in order to make them capable of reflecting and transmitting celestial light and the virtues of the spirit.

The spirit does not need to evolve. On the contrary, its role is to involute, that is, to descend into matter and animate it. In its own sublime region it is perfect. This question must be very clear in the mind of a disciple: the spirit can do anything on high, on its own level, but it is powerless on the level of matter until the organs of the physical body are ready to allow it to manifest itself. It is extremely important to understand this, for human beings are influenced turn and turn about by materialistic philosophies and false notions of spirituality, and they have great difficulty in getting the two in perspective. All the different forms used by alchemists were expressions of the one idea: that man should work on matter in order to make it more and more subtle and transmute it into gold, the symbol of perfection.[2]

So it is not so much the soul and spirit we should worry about, but the physical instruments by means of which the soul and spirit manifest themselves, and one of the most important of these, of course, is the brain. When a person is mentally deficient, it is not his spirit which is at fault; his spirit may well be that of a sage, but the instrument with which it is expected to manifest itself, the human brain, is incapable of functioning as it should. Even the greatest violinist in the world cannot play if the strings of his violin are broken or slack. And the spirit is a virtuoso violinist who needs a good instrument in order to produce good music. People expect too much of the spirit: they give it a broken-down body and expect it to do wonders. But it cannot! It is exactly as though you tried to get a spark from a damp match: it cannot be done!

The reason why human beings don't receive revelations from heaven is that they are prisoners of material concerns which weigh them down and suffocate them. It never even occurs to them to devote a few moments to making contact with the divine world or with the sun; the only thing they are interested in is how to settle this or arrange that. I am not saying that you should neglect your worldly affairs, but it is extremely important to lay aside one's preoccupations from time to time, just as one would lay aside a heavy burden. Take an example from the bearers who carry huge loads of equipment on a mountaineering expedition: from time to time they lay down their loads, breathe freely for a few minutes, sit down and refresh themselves with some food and drink, and then they load up and off they go again! Why can't you do as much?

So, from time to time, think about leaving your worries somewhere for an hour or two; I promise you no one will steal them while you're not looking; there are not many people who are eager to assume other people's burdens! So lay them down – they will still be there when you come back – and get into touch with heaven.[3]

Notes

1. See *Looking into the Invisible – Intuition, Clairvoyance, Dreams,* Izvor Coll. n° 228, chap. 15: 'Protect yourself while you are asleep', chap. 16: 'Astral projection while asleep'.
2. See *The Philosopher's Stone – in the Gospels and in Alchemy,* Izvor Coll. n° 241, chap. 9: 'The work of the alchemist: 3 over 4', chap. 10: 'The philosopher's stone, fruit of a mystic union', chap. 11: 'The regeneration of matter: the cross and the crucible'.
3. See *The Path of Silence,* Izvor Coll. n° 229, chap. 3: 'Leave your cares at the door'.

II

Not so many years ago, when people's homes were still lit by oil lamps, the glass chimneys had to be cleaned every evening. All combustion produces wastes and the oil in these lamps deposited a film of soot on the inside of the glass, so that, even if the flame was lit, the lamp gave no light unless the glass was cleaned. The same phenomenon occurs in each one of us, for life is combustion.[1] All our thoughts, feelings and acts, all our manifestations, are the result of a combustion. Now it is obvious that in order to produce the flame, the energy which animates us, something has to burn and that burning necessarily entails waste products which then have to be eliminated. Just as the lamp fails to light up the house if its glass is coated with soot; just as a wood or coal-burning stove gives less heat if it is cluttered with ashes and cinders, similarly, if a man fails to purify himself he will sink deeper and deeper into the cold and dark and end by losing life itself.

Unfortunately, human beings have never thought about these correspondences, and they imagine that they can live perfectly well without bothering about getting rid of their impurities. They know that they have to wash every day otherwise the pores of the skin get clogged up and this is bad for their health. But they never bother to wash themselves inwardly, so the pores of their spiritual skin are clogged up, no light can get through to them, they live in perpetual darkness, and then they accuse heaven of abandoning them or turning a deaf ear to their prayers.

No, no! heaven has not abandoned us, nor is it deaf to our prayers! The barriers between us are our doing; it is we who have surrounded ourselves with such dense layers, it is we who have so strengthened and consolidated the barriers, that heaven cannot get through to us. The divine World is all about us and yet we feel isolated and apart from it simply because we are so heavily wrapped up in the dense layers formed by our own baser thoughts and feelings which prevent us from feeling that presence. In reality, heaven, light and joy are all round us, within our reach, and anyone who decides to purify himself and work at making his subtle bodies more sensitive and receptive, will find that there is no such thing as a gulf between himself and heaven.

Let me illustrate this with another example. When the sky is clear we can see the sun, and then, when clouds begin to gather, they block out the sight of the sun. But if you take a plane and climb to thirty thousand feet you will find yourself above the layer of cloud, where the sun is always shining.

Well, from the esoteric point of view, the clouds are simply dense, opaque, drab thoughts and feelings, and when they gather in our hearts and minds they block out the sun. There is a sun which is always shining within us, a sun that is God Himself, the Source of life, the Source of light. It is always there, deep within us, hidden in the very core of our being, but we cannot see or feel it; we feel as though we were out in the dark, shivering with cold. Why? Because we have not learned how to purify ourselves.

It is extremely important for man to know how to eliminate impurities from his psychic bodies. This is why a disciple spends so much time on exercises of purification. And I am not thinking only about physical methods: breathing exercises, ablutions and so on; I am thinking of spiritual means of purification, concentration and prayer. For it is by means of these exercises that he introduces a special substance into himself which dissolves and washes out the foreign, harmful elements.[2]

I have repeatedly given you exercises to do, also, with the four elements: fire that burns, air that blows things away, water that washes and the earth that engulfs things. Try to find these exercises and start using them. It is in your own interest. Every day, several times a day, remember that your physical and psychic activities are the result of combustion and that they leave waste products behind them which you must get rid of. These waste products are, perhaps, no more than a thin film of smoke, but if that thin film of smoke accumulates day after day, it will end by forming a thick, black layer which you will never be able to get rid of.

Let's take yet another example from everyday life which you have never thought of interpreting. Everybody eats but everybody also has to evacuate a certain proportion of what they have eaten: this is a law which is binding on all creatures. If you study the human digestive system you will see that it has been perfectly designed to take in food and eliminate that part of it which cannot be assimilated. And if the kidneys or intestines fail to function correctly, poisoning gradually sets in. But this is true not only on the physical level; equally, on the etheric, astral and mental planes, if the eliminatory function fails, man gradually poisons himself. Countless men and women are suffering from psychic poisoning because their etheric, astral and mental bodies are overloaded with impurities! They have never learned that on those levels, too, there are elements which have to be eliminated, so all their ducts are dirty and clogged up. They need to be cleaned and unblocked so that things can start flowing again.

This is but one more proof of what I have just been saying. We are immersed in the divine, abundant, luminous life which is all around us, but we cannot feel its presence, communications have broken down because our channels are blocked up. This explains why the essential function of Initiation is to teach disciples that it is only by purification that they can restore communications and make it possible for divine life to circulate through them. When life flows freely, it brings with it all the essential elements needed by the cells of the body. When it ceases to flow death follows.

All that I have revealed to you here has been written into nature by Cosmic Intelligence, but you have never taken the trouble to decipher it. Study the lives of different kinds of creatures and you will see that, at one time or another, all of them, without exception, have to eliminate something. Every day of your lives, therefore, several times a day, think about cleansing and purifying yourself. Open up the flood gates and let the heavenly waters flow over you; picture yourself immersed in an impetuous torrent of water or under a waterfall, while all your impurities are swept away on the current. Or imagine, for instance, that you are a crystal and that, little by little, you are becoming transparent. Oh, of course, you will not become physically transparent! But if you met a clairvoyant he would be able to see that in the etheric, astral and mental dimensions of your being, you had become as pure and transparent as a crystal, he would see the celestial energies flowing through you just as light flows into a prism and out again in the form of seven rays of colour. All these methods exist, and they are very effective; so why not use them instead of continually suffering and lamenting and making yourself a nuisance to everyone else?

You must think of purifying yourself every day, for impurities come from every direction and settle on you, not only the physical impurities that you accumulate by eating, drinking and breathing, but the psychic impurities produced by your own thoughts and feelings and the thoughts and feelings of others, which can also poison you. So, keep an eye on yourself: be careful and discriminating about what you read, what you watch and the people you associate with and, above all, keep a rein on your thoughts and your daily habits, for it is only if you are vigilant in this way that you will become pure, spiritually pure. And this purity will be a source of countless blessings, not only to you yourself, but also to others; everything and everyone you meet will benefit from your purity which cleanses and illuminates them.[3]

You must never forget that your inner state is not only your own private concern but that it affects others as well. If you yourself are impure, even though you may feel the desire to help others, your emanations will sully them: you can do no good unless you are pure. So, there it is: this is an absolute and you cannot get round it! If you really want to help mankind you can do so by your purity. Even if you never say a word to anyone, your purity frees a passage for light which passes through you and contributes to the improvement of all those around you. Yes, if you are pure, your presence alone is sufficient. Equally, if you are impure, that is to say, if you are evil, unjust, greedy and lawless, you are one of those who are poisoning the entire world. You may not believe me, of course, but that does not alter the facts; I believe – or rather, I know – that this is true.

What do human beings want most? Strength, will-power, love and money – above all, money! Everybody is in the running for money! But how many are ready to put themselves out for purity? And yet purity is the foundation of everything. If you concentrate on growing in purity, all the rest will follow automatically. Purity will make you healthier, more beautiful, stronger and more intelligent. Yes, I know: our clever contemporaries who are all so learned, have totally neglected the question of purity. 'A pure life? What are you talking about? What good can that do you?' They are busy with all kinds of other things, and then, owing to the impurity of their lives, they begin to falter and fall ill and end by losing everything they have got, all because their foundations were shaky. Yes, purity is the foundation stone! There have been saints who had never opened a book or studied anything in their lives, but who concentrated all their efforts on perfecting their purity. And, lo and behold, all the other qualities began to develop as well: knowledge, clairvoyance, the power of healing, etc., simply because there were no opaque layers in them, no more barriers to the influx of all heaven's treasures.

So you must work at this every day: sweep, scrub and wash out all impurities, and clear a way for light to flood into you, as though you were professional cleaning women! 'What?' you will exclaim in horror; 'We're planning to become princes and princesses, and here you are, telling us to become charwomen!' Yes; didn't you know that a cleaning woman can become a princess? Once you have got everything clean and shining inside, you can throw off all your old rags and put on princely robes!

Notes
1. See *The Mysteries of Fire and Water,* Izvor Coll. n° 232, chap. 2: 'The secret of combustion'.
2. See *A New Earth – Methods, exercises, formulas, prayers,* Complete Works, vol. 13, chap. 6: 'Methods of purification', chap. 10: 'Mental work'.
3. See *The Wellsprings of Eternal Joy,* Izvor Coll. n° 242, chap. 11: 'Going abroad'.

Chapter Eight

LIVING WITH THE INTENSITY OF LIGHT

Light travels through space at about 300,000 kilometres a second; this means that it moves faster than anything else we know in the whole of the physical world. Why is it that Cosmic Intelligence has endowed light with a greater capacity for speed than anything else? With the exception of the initiates who, from time immemorial, have always given first place in their philosophy to light, no one has ever paused to wonder why this is, or to reflect on its consequences for the spiritual life.

Nothing can equal the speed of light, and it is this that gives it a tremendous superiority over everything else. Yes, because speed is a criterion of perfection which is not confined to purely technical things. If your mental processes slow down, for instance, if you cannot count on them to give you a rapid and accurate view of a critical situation, you may well have accidents or fall into some kind of trap. Similarly, when one's inner, psychic life slows down, everything becomes more difficult. Yes: light is a yardstick, a criterion.

Light is unencumbered, disinterested, totally without selfish thoughts or desires; it is not weighed down by all kinds of false notions, and this is why it can move so fast: it always comes in first! If you are interested in exploring the human heart, the wide universe, all the wealth of the universal Soul, you must know that you can only do so on condition that you are capable of acting with the speed and intensity of light.

It is the intensity of vibrations of the matter of which they are composed which differentiates and distinguishes the various kingdoms of the universe from each other. From the mineral to the human kingdoms and beyond, through all the angelic hierarchies all the way to the throne of God, life manifests itself with increasing intensity and subtlety.[1] One could say that the degree of evolution of a being can be judged by the intensity of its life. Most human beings who have not understood this, live in slow motion: their hearts, lungs, livers and brains, their mental processes; everything in them stagnates, and they don't know that there is nothing more dangerous. When a man lives in slow motion it is as though he were driving his car in bottom gear down a muddy lane: all the mud sticks to the wheels; but if he accelerates, the wheels spin faster and throw off the mud. It is so easy to understand that one wonders why so many human 'wheels' move so sluggishly.

People are labouring under the delusion that, because they know what it is to experience great emotional stress, anger or the delights of sleeping with someone, they know what it is to live with intensity! No, tears, angry gestures or transports of passion do not prove the intensity of life. A truly intense life is almost imperceptible. He who lives life with intensity may make no outward movement at all, but inwardly he may be vibrating at the speed of light or even faster. For, although it is true that light is faster than anything else on the physical level, on the etheric, astral and mental levels, man can reach much greater speeds: by means of his thought and his spirit, which are forms of light, he can move at a speed of millions of kilometres per second. The light of the sun takes about eight minutes to reach the earth, whereas thought can reach the farthest point of space in a flash. The spirit, therefore, can move far more rapidly than light, and yet light is still the best example of speed we can have to show us that we must live our lives with greater intensity.

If you apply the criterion of the speed with which light vibrates to all the circumstances of your life, your reasoning will be truer, you will reflect more clearly and you will have a more reliable basis on which to found an analysis of everything that goes on in your inner life. And this is important, for when you have experienced some particularly sublime moments you should be able to judge whether or not you can maintain that exalted state of consciousness. You have all noticed that there are days when a certain piece of music thrills you and transports you to the seventh heaven, and on other days it barely moves you at all. Well, you should be aware of this kind of reaction in all the other areas of your psychic life as well; you must learn to recognize the intensity of your emotions. Lovers are perhaps the only ones who are capable of saying whether it was the first or the last kiss that was the most intense. They, at least, have some criteria to go by! Well, let's put it like that, anyway, without going into it!

So, a disciple must discern what goes on inside himself and, particularly in regard to his meditations, recognize whether his level of consciousness has increased in subtlety and intensity, in other words, in spirituality, or whether, on the contrary, it has slipped back into low gear. For this is another of the great qualities that you must develop: your discernment. You should be in a position to know, day by day, month by month and year by year, whether you have made progress, whether you have reached a higher level by comparison with the day or the month or the year before. There is a tremendous diversity of events and elements in the psychic life, so there are always thousands of things to be studied, analysed and classified.

It is when you live with intensity every single day that you will make all kinds of new discoveries about your inner life, for that intensity constantly reveals something new. Perhaps you will say, 'But how can you make discoveries in yourself? I quite see that if you read or study you'll find out things you never knew before; but can you really discover anything new in yourself?' Yes, indeed you can! A life lived with intensity is the path that leads to the essential truths of the universe. You will never discover these truths if they do not spring from within, if you have not actually experienced them in your life. Obviously, if you have someone who can reveal them to you – especially if it is someone you love and trust – that is excellent, but even then you are going to have to ascertain each truth for yourself.

If men and women are perpetually in the grip of uncertainty and doubt, it is because they look for truth outside themselves, and one can never be absolutely sure of something that is external to oneself.[2] The inner route is the only one which makes doubt impossible. Even if you wanted to doubt your inner experience you could not do so: when you have toothache, for instance, do you doubt it? Do you say, 'Just a moment... let me see... does it hurt or doesn't it? Yes? No? Maybe?' Unfortunately, this is one of those cases where doubt is impossible! We can always be sure of what we experience in our inner sanctum. And this is why the only authentic discoveries are those which spring from our inner life when it is as intense, strong and radiant as light. This is the life that we must wish and pray for, and for which we must prepare ourselves so that it can come and dwell within us.

Take the example of what happens in the mornings, at sunrise: if you are just sitting there, looking at the sun and feeling rather bored, you will end by going to sleep. But if you are wide awake and intensely alive, your whole being will begin to vibrate as you feel the sun on you. If your life is not intense you will really know neither the sun nor the stars, neither God nor the Bible, nor even those you love.

So what do you have to do to begin living your lives with intensity? Well, the first thing to do is to accept the idea and understand that this intensity is something very desirable and advantageous; secondly you must begin to love and long for it, and, finally, you must make up your minds to give it concrete reality. If you do this, all the rest will follow on little by little. The really important thing is to begin by accepting the idea of living with intensity, because until you do this you will continue to live in slow motion and to stagnate. In fact, there are people who receive inspirations from heaven and who do everything in their power to shut them out, under the pretext that it is not normal! Do they think it would be better to be like stones? A lot of people distrust and try to avoid any contact with divine currents from heaven simply because some ignorant person has told them that they could be dangerous and send them out of their minds! Since when has an intense spiritual life led to insanity? I ask you! Do you think that all those who are in the psychiatric wards have been brought to that pass by an intense, divine spiritual life? Or by their disordered passions?[3]

If light can move so swiftly it is because it is disinterested; it has only the noblest and best intentions in its head. You are probably a little surprised because you have never heard anyone suggest that light had a head! Yes, light can move so fast because it has freed itself from everything base, animal or even human; it has no burdens. Have you ever seen a man with a heavy load on his back, running fast? It can't be done. If you want to run you have to be free and unhampered by any heavy loads. And light, you see, is very intelligent: it has never wanted to assume any useless burdens or stupid obligations that would hold it back. It has always wanted to be free, and that is why it can move so fast, and, my goodness, how it can go!

And as light is also full of love, it is in a hurry to help human beings; its love urges it to move very fast so as to be useful at once. Other people, who are slowed down by all kinds of burdens, get there when the patient is already dead! They hear that someone is dying, and a hundred years later they turn up to try and save his life: that is how fast human beings are! But light is more intelligent than anything or anyone.

The ideal of a disciple is to free himself from all restrictions, to throw off everything that hampers him, and become like light. Of course, this is not as easy as all that! As long as one is still living in the material world one is always tied down by interdictions and obligations. But he who is conscious and decides to take light as his guide, begins to free himself and to vibrate so intensely that nothing can hold him back: he flies through space, visiting and observing everything and, thanks to his inner swiftness, he is able to discover all the hidden marvels of the universe. Compare someone like this to those who have no ambition to move out of their rut: they have never travelled; they have never left their village; they spend their whole life with their pigs and cows and sheep – what can they possibly tell us? They have never visited or seen anything, whereas light goes everywhere and sees everything that is going on, it is constantly learning; so we should address all our questions to light, and ask it to tell us what it has seen and learned on its travels. But we are a long way from using methods of this kind: nobody thinks of asking a sunbeam what it has seen or what it has brought back from all the places it has visited. Still less does anyone decide to behave like a sunbeam!

Every morning, at sunrise, you have the ideal conditions for beginning to live your life with intensity. But before you can do this, you must learn to free yourself from greed for material things, for you can increase the intensity of your thoughts and feelings and begin to travel through space only if you are content with very little in the way of material goods. Jesus was familiar with this law, and expressed it by saying that it was easier for a camel to go through the eye of a needle than for a rich man to enter into the kingdom of God. At first sight this is a ridiculous thing to say: how could a big, bulky camel ever go through the eye of a needle and a little runt of a rich man be unable to go through a huge gateway? The answer given by initiatic science, of course, is that Jesus was talking not about the physical, but about the astral body: when the astral body is swollen by all kinds of material desires man cannot enter into the kingdom of heaven; he cannot get through the door! Whereas a camel symbolizes a being whose astral body is very slim because he lives abstemiously and is content with just enough food and water to cross the desert.[4]

Yes, all initiates are in agreement about this: the more deeply committed man is to worldly affairs, the less opportunity he will have of living with intensity and learning to vibrate in unison with light. Just look at all those tycoons who want to swallow up the whole world! True, they make a lot of noise, issue streams of orders and run all over the world: there is no denying that their activity is intense. But that is not the kind of intensity I am talking about. The truly intense life does not manifest itself in words, gestures and movement. If you live with the intensity of light you can just be there quite quietly, without moving a muscle, and yet be in touch with the heart of the universe. But you can only understand this if you actually achieve it. It is as difficult to put into words as it is to express those rare moments when a man and woman who love each other, exchange a wordless look that will stay in their hearts for ever. Not a word, not a gesture passes between them; but nothing could ever convey the intensity of the love expressed in that stillness. Whereas others go down on their knees, stuttering and stammering, 'I love you. I adore you! Your eyes, your hair, your smile... I'll give you heaven itself. I'd willingly die for you!' Oh, what a din! You want nothing better than to send him off with a flea in his ear!

But, dear Lord, isn't that what I'm doing all the time? I never stop talking and explaining, talking and explaining. What a job! But I am looking forward to the day when I need not say anything any more, when we can just be here, together, in a silence of such extraordinary quality! Yes, but you have to be prepared for this. You still need more preparation in order to be capable of receiving, experiencing and understanding all that I could give you in that way.[5]

You see, I have this great body of knowledge, this tremendous programme that I am following. Some of you are not very pleased about that: they would like me to talk differently, to speak about other subjects or decide to do things differently. I know that lecturers in the world always try to satisfy the desires of their public, but the question is quite different in my case: my programme is based on something completely different from the tastes and preferences of people who are not always very enlightened; so if they are not happy about it, that's too bad, but it just cannot be helped! I shall never agree to the suggestions of those who want me to give them more book-learning. They are far too used to using their intellect without ever putting anything into practice: they don't pray, they don't meditate, they never do any exercises and they are doing nothing to transform themselves. All they are interested in is knowledge: they read, they record, they make enquiries and keep themselves informed about current events. But that is not the best way to evolve and free oneself – and they will find this out one day – for they never do anything concrete, they never put all that knowledge into practice in their gestures, their acts, their general behaviour.

People know everything and do nothing! They know that patience can work miracles but they are not patient. They know that with gentleness one can obtain extraordinary results, but they are always flying into a rage. They know, they know, they know... but when it comes to putting all that knowledge into effect they seem to lose interest. Well, they can please themselves, but that is no way to transform themselves; on the contrary, if they go on like that they will always be weak and vulnerable, drab, sickly and unhappy. They will never know what it means to live with intensity.

Notes
1. See *Angels and other Mysteries of The Tree of Life,* Izvor Coll. n° 236, chap. 1: 'From man to God, the notion of hierarchy'
2. See *Truth: Fruit of Wisdom ad Love,* Izvor Coll. n° 234, chap. 1: 'The quest for truth', and *The Faith That Moves Mountains,* Izvor Coll. n° 238, chap. 3: 'Faith and belief'.

3. See *La pédagogie initiatique,* Complete Works, vol. 28, chap. 1: 'Pourquoi choisir la vie spirituelle?'.
4. See *'Et il me montra un fleuve d'eau de la vie',* Synopsis Coll., Part VIII, chap. 1: 'Entrez par la porte étroite'.
5. See *The Path of Silence,* Izvor Coll. n° 229, chap. 11: 'A Master speaks in silence'.

Chapter Nine

THE SPIRITUAL LASER

I

On the technical level, light has many absolutely extraordinary possibilities which ancient civilizations, such as that of Atlantis, knew long before our time. We know, for instance, that they used to collect and condense the light of the sun by means of huge crystals, and that they used the energy obtained in this way to run all kinds of instruments and machines. In our day, scientists have invented the Laser, by means of which light is concentrated into a single beam of tremendous power which can be used to perform all kinds of extraordinary operations. But I don't intend to talk to you about the technical applications of the laser beam; what I want to talk about is its application to the spiritual life.

As you know, the word LASER is formed from the initial letters of 'Light Amplification by Stimulated Emission of Radiation,' and the technique was developed by the American physicist Theodor Maiman in 1960 or thereabouts. The laser consists of a cylindrical synthetic ruby crystal which is silvered at one end to make a reflecting mirror, and partially silvered at the other to make a semi-reflecting mirror. The crystal is surrounded by a spiral flash lamp which, when switched on, raises the chromium atoms in the ruby to an excited state (a process which is known as optical stimulation). When the stimulation is sufficiently intense, a narrow beam of extremely powerful light is emitted from the semi-reflecting end of the crystal.

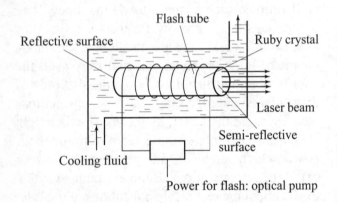

Figure 1. Diagram of a simple ruby laser

The laser produces light with all the waves of the same wavelength (i.e. monochromatic), which is emitted in the same direction and the same phase (i.e. coherent), and it is precisely for this reason that it is of such great interest, for monochromatic coherent light is extraordinarily powerful. I shall not go into technical details here; you can look them up for yourselves in a manual of physics if you want to. What interests me is to show you how, thousands of years before our modern scientists discovered the laser, the initiates already knew and used it.

Figure 2. The caduceus of Hermes

The principle of the laser can be seen in the caduceus of Hermes, which is, in turn, a representation of man (Figure 2). The central wand represents man's spine and the two intertwined snakes represent the two currents that descend from the two hemispheres of the brain. These currents cross over on the level of the nape of the neck, pass on down through the lungs, cross over again at the solar plexus, continue downwards through the spleen and liver, cross over again on the level of the navel, pass through the left and right kidneys, cross again at the Hara chakra and, finally, pass through the genital glands of a man and the ovaries of a woman (Figure 3).

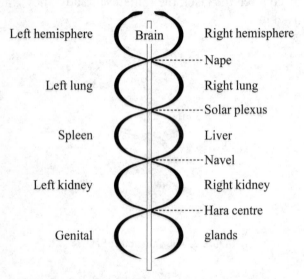

Figure 3. The path taken by the two currents

In point of fact, it is not two snakes which are intertwined round the central magic wand, but one, and this one is polarized both positively and negatively. The wand always stands for the masculine principle and the serpent, the spiral, stands for the feminine principle which entwines itself round the masculine principle in order to heighten and intensify its powers. This is the underlying meaning of the caduceus of Hermes. The central rod represents the mental dimension whereas the polarized serpent represents the astral dimension, for, as I have already explained, the astral plane is criss-crossed by two currents: one that rises and another that descends. The caduceus of Hermes, therefore, is a symbol of the two principles, symbolized by the caduceus: the masculine principle represented by the wand, and the feminine principle represented by the snake which is positively and negatively polarized, for the feminine principle is always expressed by the number 2. The caduceus represents man, with all the innate powers and possibilities which he must develop in order to manifest divine power.

The caduceus of Hermes can also be seen, in another form, in the sephirotic Tree of Life, with its two lateral pillars, the pillar of Severity (positive) and the pillar of Mercy (negative), on either side of the central pillar of Equilibrium. Two currents descend from *Kether,* pass through *Chokmah* and *Binah,* cross over at *Daath,* pass through *Chesed* and *Geburah,* cross over again at *Tiphareth,* pass through *Netzach* and *Hod* and, finally, cross over again at *Yesod* which symbolically represents the generative organs[1] (Figure 4).

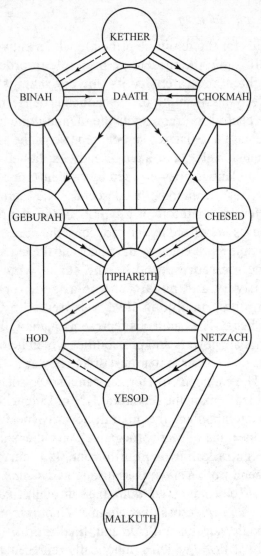

Figure 4 The sephirotic Tree of Life

According to Hindu tradition, man has three etheric canals running the length of his spinal cord: in the centre is *Sushumna,* on the left is *Ida* and on the right, *Pingala*. By means of various appropriate bodily postures, breathing exercises and meditation, Indian yogis awaken *kundalini,* the latent energy which lies at the base of the spine in the chakra *Muladara*. This energy, which is compared to a coiled serpent, rises by the canal of *Sushumna,* passing through each chakra in turn: S*vadhisthana, Manipura, Anahata, Visuddha* and *Ajna,* awakening them as it goes, until it reaches *Sahasrara,* the chakra on the top of the head, from which it emerges in the form of a ray of light (see Figure 5). A yogi who succeeds in directing *kundalini* all the way to the *Sahasrara* chakra possesses supreme powers. But, of course, before he can reach this stage, he has to subject himself to an exceedingly strict discipline, and, in fact, in spite of this discipline, very few yogis ever manage to send their *kundalini* energy up to *Sahasrara.*

There have been cases in which someone who was insufficiently prepared, who had not purified himself or acquired sufficient self-mastery, aroused kundalini prematurely or by accident, and was struck down by it, for it is an overwhelming force which can destroy anyone who is incapable of mastering it, not only psychically but even physically. So it is more prudent not to try and arouse

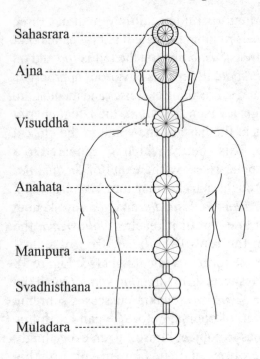

Figure 5. The seven chakras

kundalini energy prematurely. However, someone
who has spent years preparing himself can do so in
perfect safety, and one of the most effective ways
is by breathing exercises, for the nostrils are
connected with the two currents, *Ida* (feminine)
and *Pingala* (masculine). When these two currents
are stimulated by breathing exercises, they, in turn,
stimulate *kundalini* (also known as the green fire),

which rises through the spinal cord, stimulating the electrons as it goes, until it reaches the brain, where it unites with the masculine principle, Siva. This is the union of the two principles, the supreme triumph, and the initiate who achieves this becomes capable of emitting fire.[2]

We see, therefore, how the Hebrew, Greek and Hindu traditions use different symbolic forms to describe the same spiritual process in man, which modern science has now rediscovered in its technical applications, with the laser. Actually, the scientists who make these revolutionary discoveries are reincarnations of ancient Atlanteans. For the Atlanteans knew all about the laser and various other techniques recently discovered, as well as many others which still remain to be rediscovered.

But, I say again, science simply adapts certain phenomena which already exist in man, and applies them on the technical level. Let me give you just one example. Before I do so, however, I must warn you that some of you may be shocked, so you will understand if I imitate the judge who addressed the spectators at a trial, saying, 'Ladies and gentlemen, in view of the scandalous nature of the facts we must now expose, I invite anyone who may be shocked to leave the court.' After a short pause, during which no one moved, the judge said, 'Now that those whose finer feelings are shocked by indecency have left, we may resume the trial!' So, now that all the 'prudes' have left, this is what I want to tell you: that which takes place between a man and woman during the sexual act can be compared to the laser. The man's organ is heated and stimulated by that of the woman, and the resultant light is a ray of such power that it creates a child! The male organ plays the part of the ruby rod and the female organ that of the spiral flash. So science never actually invents anything: it discovers and adapts truths which have existed in nature from all eternity.

Until very recently, although scientists had obtained a number of important results by means of light, they had not yet been in a position to exploit all of its possibilities, because there was no known way of producing a beam of monochromatic coherent light. Now that this has been achieved it will prove to be the point of departure for numbers of fantastic realizations.

It is a pity, though, that it did not occur to the physicists to bend the ruby rod into an S-shape, similar to that of the human backbone; if they had done so they would have obtained even more sensational results. You will probably say that the shape makes no difference, but that is just where you are wrong: it does! Why do you suppose that light, and waves in general, flow with a sinusoidal movement? And what currents have given the backbone this S-shape? You will probably say that the reason is mechanical: it is the most functionally efficient form for its work, that is, to provide support for the head, limbs and organs of the body. Ah, yes: people always think of the mechanical reasons – but there are others... However, we had better leave that question for another time.

Light is all-powerful. God created light before anything else and it is the source of everything else. But human beings don't know how to work with light. Even the mystics who are always talking about light don't really know how to use it. And now it has fallen to scientists to surpass the mystics and demonstrate the power of light. The future will be one great discovery of light!

Unfortunately, while scientists are conducting their experiments in well-equipped laboratories, they neglect their own inner laboratories equipped for them by nature. And yet, with the more perfect equipment of these inner laboratories, they would be in a position to produce phenomena far more spectacular than anything they achieve on the physical level. Why should everything be so splendid on the outside of man and not within him? A lot of people are anxious for you to go and see their workshop, their factory or their studio, but they would never think of inviting you to go and see their inner sanctum, because they know that it is in a state of wild disorder, and that their passions are roaming loose and unbridled within them. It is nothing to be proud of, you would not be impressed, so it is better to keep it hidden. But, all the same, it is a pity!

Notes
1. See *Cosmic Balance – The Secret of Polarity,* Izvor Coll. n° 237, chap. 9: 'The caduceus of Hermes – The astral serpent'.
2. See *Man's Subtle Bodies and Centres – the Aura, the Solar Plexus, the Chakras...,* Izvor Coll. n° 219, chap. 5: 'Kundalini force', chap. 6: 'The chakras'.

As I have already said, although the laser has actually been built only very recently, initiates have known the principle of it for thousands of years, for nothing can be discovered on the physical plane which does not already exist, in some form or another, on a subtler level. Man does not really discover or invent anything. To 'discover' something is simply to uncover, by means of intuition or imagination or by groping in the dark, something that already exists on a subtler level.[1] Things like radio, television and telephones are all constructed in accordance with the same laws as those which govern not only the higher planes, but also our own physical bodies: our ears and eyes, brain, heart and lungs, etc.

I have already shown you how the laser principle exists in man: the spine (which is vertical), and the male sexual organ (which, when it is active, is horizontal), are two kinds of laser. When an initiate wants to sublimate his sexual energy, he does not restrict his work to the lower laser, the sexual organ; he works with the vertical laser, the spinal column which is far more powerful; it can move heaven and earth. So, the question for a disciple is how to move from the horizontal to the vertical. The horizontal is the line of matter, the vertical that of the spirit and the cross is the synthesis of the two. Ask any Christian what the cross means and you will see: he will not be able to tell you. The cross only means something to Christians because Jesus was crucified, but in fact, it is a symbol with far greater significance.[2]

But let's get back to the laser. If a disciple really wants to make the passage from the horizontal laser to the vertical laser he must cease to regard the sexual act solely as a source of pleasure, and learn to see it as a form of work. Very often, when men and women come to me, complaining that they are incapable of controlling their sexual energy, I have to explain that it is because it is associated in their minds with the idea of pleasure rather than that of work. Sexual energy flows from the same source as the energy of the sun; it is 'The strength of all strengths' of which Hermes Trismegistus speaks, and which exists on every plane: on the physical plane it manifests itself as sexual energy, and on the spiritual plane it manifests itself as pure light.

Since man is a replica of the universe, he who is able to direct this energy up to his brain, to the *Sahasrara* chakra, emits a form of light which is identical with the light of the sun, whereas when those who use the canal of the lower laser emit light, it condenses and becomes a liquid. But whatever form it takes, this energy is still of the same nature as that of the sun. An initiate who has reached the point of purifying every single cell of his body, is capable of emitting etheric particles from his sexual organ, a kind of invisible light which produces beneficial effects on every created being.

You will probably exclaim in horror: 'What you are saying is absolutely indecent!' Well, there are many things which may seem indecent to those who have never learned to read and interpret the book of living nature with purity and disinterestedness. In point of fact, even that which man gives to a woman in sexual intercourse, on the physical plane, varies in quality according to his degree of evolution. For, you must realize that, generally speaking, the way in which a person lives determines the quality of his emanations.

Human beings have such a crude materialistic conception of things that, for them, the only forms of exchange worth mentioning between men and women, are those in which they kiss and cuddle and sleep together. But this is a very false view: actually, although they are not always aware of it, men and women exchange many subtler things on a far higher plane. In a social gathering, for instance, a boy and girl who are complete strangers may glimpse each other through the throng and feel suddenly drawn to each other: when this happens, a certain part of the boy's body emits something etheric which, without either of them being really aware of it, is picked up by the girl and surges through her whole body. They haven't kissed, they haven't even touched, and yet, when they get home that night they have an overwhelming sense that something wonderful has happened to them, simply because, unknowingly, the boy has given the girl something and she, equally unknowingly, has received the gift.

As I have said, this energy is of the same nature as solar energy. Obviously, the disordered, chaotic lives of most men prevent it from having the purity of sunlight, but in an initiate who is very close to perfection it is an energy that can have a beneficial effect on the whole of nature and even on other human beings. This is a delicate question, because one is never quite sure of how one's words will be understood. What would happen if some people were to take it into their heads, from what I have said, that they are as pure as the sun? That is why I insist that you must not allow yourselves to entertain all kinds of extravagant ideas in this connection. If I explain how Cosmic Intelligence has conceived man in the likeness of the sun, it is in order to stimulate you in your work, and it is up to you to understand me correctly and to give all your efforts a spiritual orientation.

In any case, as you well know, I am not opposed to love: all I am saying is that you must choose the most worthy aspects, the highest manifestations of love, that is all. Love is the only thing that has the power to lead mankind to perfection, but if it is not correctly understood and manifested, instead of perfecting humanity it can lead to its ruin.

This 'strength of all strengths' is sexual energy, for what other form of energy is there in the whole universe to compare to it? Besides, Hermes Trismegistus tells us that it comes from the sun: 'The father thereof is the sun.' The sad thing is, though, that man has so debased and defiled himself that there is nothing sun-like in the act by which men fertilize women. However, it is destined to recapture that likeness, and not only the sexual act, but all the acts of our daily lives, must become sun-like, that is to say, luminous, warm and life-giving.

In the sephirotic Tree, *Kether* is linked to the Father, *Tiphareth* to the Son and *Yesod* to the Holy Spirit. When I talked to you about the 'Mysteries of *Yesod'*, I told you that it was there, in *Yesod,* that pure love was to be found, and that this is why the *'blasphemy against the Holy Spirit'* mentioned in the Gospels, is the blasphemy against love.[3] The Holy Spirit is that energy which is love, that energy which, when it springs from purity, takes the upward path. *Kundalini* is simply the fire of the Holy Spirit dormant in man. And it is through purity, and purity alone, that it awakens in *Yesod,* rises to *Tiphareth,* the heart, where it becomes light and thence to *Kether,* the Crown chakra, where it becomes omnipotence.[4]

So kundalini-force is identical with that 'strength of all strengths' of which Hermes Trismegistus speaks. This force, which is capable of creating life is a condensation of the light of the sun. In an initiate who manages to sublimate it, it returns to its etheric state and manifests as light shining through his eyes and brain.

Notes
1. See *The Faith That Moves Mountains,* Izvor Coll. n° 238, chap. 6: 'Retrieving lost knowledge'.
2. See *The Symbolic Language of Geometrical Figures,* Izvor Coll. n° 218, chap. 6: 'The cross'.
3. See *'Au commencement était le Verbe',* Complete Works, vol. 9, chap. 10: 'Le péché contre le Saint-Esprit est le péché contre l'amour'.
4. See *Love and Sexuality,* Complete Works, vol. 14, chap. 9: 'From Yesod to Kether: the path of sexual sublimation'.

III

You who are seeking to reach perfection in the three worlds, physical, spiritual and divine; you who seek love, wisdom and truth; you who seek freedom, power and happiness, you must know that you will never find them unless you fix your sights on one, and only one, goal in life, unless you walk in only one direction. Whatever your duties and responsibilities may be, all your powers, all your thoughts and desires, and even the movements of your bodily cells, must be directed to that one goal: the kingdom of God and His justice; divine Love and Light. When you achieve this mobilization and unification of all your inner energies it produces such potency that you become capable of obtaining all your desires.

Every human being possesses a spirit, a soul, an intellect, a heart, a will and a physical body, and the great difficulty lies in getting them all to work in unison with each other. No one can be strong or powerful until he achieves inner unity, and one of the goals of initiation is to create this harmony in man. This is why I keep insisting on the necessity of getting all your faculties and all your activities to converge towards a single target. Whether it be your soul or your spirit, your intellect or your heart, your stomach or your sex, you must orientate them all towards that one goal: the illumination and perfecting of your whole being. Once you have achieved this unity in yourselves, we shall be able to concentrate on light when we are all here, together, and release such power that, if I give you some special formulas to say, it will have beneficial effects on the whole of mankind.

Yes, indeed; I wish I could get you to understand that if we do our mental work correctly when we are all here, together, we shall be capable of emitting light as powerful as the laser, and making its effects felt throughout the whole world.

Of course, you can do this exercise at home and concentrate on light when you are alone, but when we do it together the power is considerably amplified. If we want to reach the whole of humanity and help all men, we need a laser formed by a great many people, all concentrating on the same idea. You often complain that your meditations don't seem to produce any results: well, this is simply because you all concentrate on different subjects and, sometimes, in fact, on subjects that are so far beyond your reach that your meditation cannot possibly be efficacious. Whereas if you all concentrated on light – that is not difficult, after all; you all know what light is – each one of you would feel the support of the others and we would produce one single vibration of indescribable potency, for every one of us would be vibrating on the same wavelength as light. But there is still one thing that is missing, though, and that is the habit of concentration; only a few of you have ever really practised or are in the habit of doing the work I am talking about. As for the rest of you – the Lord alone knows what you think about! Your thoughts are scattered – forever scattered and strewn all over the place.

I have often spoken to you about the Pyramids and the symbolic meaning of the pyramidal form, with its four angles converging at the summit.[1] Well, those who built the Pyramids in the past possessed the secret of the laser. The pyramid is an invitation to man to strive for the summit, to vibrate in unison with the summit, for it is in this way that he releases untold spiritual forces. The pyramid has the same symbolic meaning as the circle with the point in the centre about which I have also spoken a great deal.[2] All strength is concentrated in this one, central point; it represents our higher self, our spirit, God Himself; whereas the surrounding circle represents our lower nature, our physical body, matter which needs to be animated by the vibrations of the spirit. By concentrating on light, whose vibrations are extremely rapid, we come closer to the central point, to God, and it is He who breathes life into our matter. It is because it vibrates with such intensity that the point is capable of forming the circle, the universe.

None of the other means you are in the habit of using to maintain your health, balance and happiness, are nearly as effective as light. Oh, I know: you are going to say that you don't believe me, because you have already tried to concentrate on light, and it did you no good at all, whereas certain pills or tablets – you only have to swallow one and, within minutes, you feel fine again! Well, let me tell you that you have drawn the wrong conclusions from your experience! You have not yet learned to work correctly with light so, of course, it is not effective. But if you learn to vibrate in unison with light, if you learn to draw it into you and make it live within you, you will soon see what it is capable of doing! Nothing can be of greater help to you than light.

All my life I have been fascinated by light; it was the only thing that interested me. That does not mean that I have fully understood it or that I possess it yet. No, but I was still very young and living in the direst poverty when I began to understand that I could not go wrong in attaching great importance to light, for it is thanks to light that we can work the most tremendous transformations not only in our physical bodies, but also in our hearts, souls and spirits and, eventually, in other people.

So many people come and see me and complain that they are discouraged and unhappy for this or that reason – or for no reason at all! And I tell them, 'The fact that you are in such a state indicates that you have not understood anything about our Teaching.' 'What do you mean?' they say, in high indignation; 'I understand every word! I've read all the books.' 'Well,' I reply; 'The simple fact that you are so upset for such ridiculous reasons shows that you have not understood any of it. To have read all my books is no proof that you have understood the Teaching. The only way that you can prove that you have understood what you have read is by putting it into practice. In fact, if you can give me that kind of concrete proof, even if you have never read a line of my books, I would say that you are a wonderful disciple!' So, if you think that light is ineffectual, it is because you do not understand it and do not know how to work with it.

Of course, when I talk to you about light in this way, you must be sure to remember what I have already explained about the two kinds of light: *svetlina*, the physical light that we can see, and *videlina*, the spiritual, primeval light created by

God on the first day, when He said, *'Let there be light!'* It was only on the fourth day, when God created the sun and moon and stars, that *svetlina* appeared as a more material manifestation of *videlina*. And the sun – which is not a ball of fire, as most people think, but a living, conscious entity – the sun receives the subtle invisible light, *videlina*, and transforms it into visible light, *svetlina*, thanks to which it shines for the whole universe. It is this quintessence of light, *videlina*, that is so powerful that if someone were to concentrate only one billionth of a milligram within himself he would overcome every obstacle.

Although this light is everywhere in space and permeates everything that exists, man cannot see or feel it because his spiritual faculties are not yet sufficiently developed to perceive a reality as subtle as this. But if he often spends time concentrating on this light, he will refine his perceptions to such a degree that, not only will he begin to feel its presence, but he will attract it to himself and it will work great transformations in him. This is why, when we have a few minutes of meditation together, you must get into the habit of putting all your preoccupations to one side and concentrating on heavenly light. In this way you will attract it and draw it into yourself so that all the worn-out particles of your body are gradually replaced by pure particles of light. In doing this exercise you are working for your own salvation, for eternal life. You must never cease your search for light, for it is the only thing that can restore perfect harmony within you.

You can do this exercise with light in rhythm with your respiration. As you breathe in, imagine that you are drawing in light and, as you breathe out, that you are radiating it into your whole being, into every cell and every organ. Then, once more, you breathe in... and breathe out. In... out, and so on. You will very quickly feel the beneficial effects of this exercise; you will feel yourself relaxed and in peace.

Once you are brimming over with light, you can do another exercise: you breathe in light and then, as you breathe out, you imagine that you are sending it out into the whole world. Obviously, you can only do this second exercise after you have practised the first one for a very long time, and replaced a lot of your lacklustre, unhealthy particles with particles of light. You must wait until you can feel that the work of transformation and purification has taken effect before you can venture to give others the light you have received. This work with light is symbolized by the Hebrew letter *Aleph* א. *Aleph* represents the initiate who receives the heavenly light, divine life, in order to pass it on to all men.[3]

So, for just a few minutes, while we are meditating, put aside all your cares and worries.

You can pick them up again later, but for the moment, leave them at the door and tell them to wait until you have finished concentrating on light. And then I can collect all those rays of light radiating from you, condense them into one powerful beam and project it out into the whole world.

On the pretext that they don't have the right conditions or that they have not received any special gifts or talents, a lot of people think they are justified in leading a thoroughly mediocre life. No, no one has the right to make such excuses. Even if you are the most underprivileged person in all the world, from every point of view, you can still work with light; it is something which is easy and readily accessible to everyone. And when you do that work, you are doing something more important and more useful than all the work in other areas done by all the most efficient and capable people in the world. Even the poorest of the poor are capable of acquiring this higher level of consciousness and of working to help, enlighten, sustain and bring peace to the whole of mankind.

Some of you will perhaps say, 'That's utterly beyond me. It's just not possible; there are too many people in the world, and I don't amount to anything!' If you reason like that you are diminishing the value of what you are doing. Obviously, you are not going to bring about the kingdom of

God and His justice from one day to the next, but
as long as you really want it you will direct all your
strength and all your energies towards that goal.[4]
And the first results of your work will be in
yourself: it will elevate and ennoble you and, as
every phenomenon triggers certain consequences,
in one way or another, you will be bound to have a
favourable influence on others.

Henceforth, therefore, instead of scattering and
wasting our energies by concentrating on different
subjects, we would do much better to concentrate
on light so as to produce one, powerful vibration.
And when we do this exercise we can picture the
light of the sun: brilliantly white, dazzling and
transparent and if we do it, as I have explained, to
the rhythm of our breathing, we shall be generating
tremendous spiritual energy and awakening the
consciences of millions of individuals in the world,
so that all men begin to work for the peace and
happiness of mankind.

Notes

1. See *The Symbolic Language of Geometrical Figures,* Izvor
   Coll. n° 218, chap. 5: 'The pyramid'.
2. Op. cit., chap. 2: 'The circle'.
3. See *'Cherchez le Royaume de Dieu et sa Justice',* Synopsis
   Coll., Part II, chap. 2-I: 'L'alphabet cosmique. Aleph'.
4. Op. cit., Part IV, chap. 1: 'Le Royaume de Dieu et sa
   Justice'.

BIBLICAL REFERENCES

Printed in November 2009
by VASTI-DUMAS Imprimeurs
42004 Saint-Etienne – France
Imprimeur n° V002846-00F

Dépôt légal: novembre 2009
1er dépôt légal dans la même collection en france: 1983